KATE ROBERTS & MAGGIE BEATTIE ROBERTS

LITERACY

Teaching Tools for Differentiation, Rigor, and Independence

HEINEMANN
Portsmouth, NH

Heinemann

361 Hanover St.

Portsmouth, NH 03801–3912

www.heinemann.com

Offices and agents throughout the world

The authors and publisher wish to thank those who have generously given permission to reprint borrowed material:

Figure 3–8: Image of monkey in cage © Don Couch/HRW Photo/HIP, bullying photos © Shutterstock/HIP, and homeless sign © Victoria Smith/Houghton Mifflin Harcourt/HIP.

Library of Congress Cataloging-in-Publication Data

Names: Roberts, Kate, author. | Roberts, Maggie Beattie, author.

Title: DIY literacy : teaching tools for differentiation, rigor, and independence / Kate Roberts, Maggie Beattie Roberts.

Description: Portsmouth, NH : Heinemann, 2016. | Includes bibliographical references.

Identifiers: LCCN 2015046898 | ISBN 9780325078168

Subjects: LCSH: Reading (Elementary). | Literacy—Study and teaching (Elementary). | Individualized reading instruction.

Classification: LCC LB1573 .R5685 2016 | DDC 372.4—dc23

LC record available at http://lccn.loc.gov/2015046898

Acquisitions editor: Tobey Antao

Production editor: Elizabeth Valway

Cover and interior designs: Monica Ann Crigler

Cover illustration: GraphicStock

Typesetter: Eric Rosenbloom, Kirby Mountain Composition

Manufacturing: Steve Bernier

Printed in the United States of America on acid-free paper

20 19 18 17 16   VP   1 2 3 4 5

To Lucy Calkins and our colleagues at the Reading and Writing Project, past and present.

We would not be who we are without you.

Contents

Foreword

Have you ever watched a home improvement show and been amazed by the transformation of the room in such a short time? It always seems impossible that anyone can transform a room in just a few days. But when I sit back and think about how these changes happen so quickly, I realize that it is often because key structures are already in place and the people making the changes have the right tools to make it happen. Changes are so much more doable with the right tools.

This is exactly how I felt when I read *DIY Literacy: Teaching Tools for Differentiation, Rigor, and Independence* by Kate Roberts and Maggie Beattie Roberts. In this book, Kate and Maggie show us how to change our workshops in significant ways with the right tools to support student learning. The book is filled with suggestions that will make a huge difference in the overall learning for our students.

I always go into the school year with a vision for how workshop will look and how students will access texts and grow at their own pace. But every year, there is a moment in the midst of a workshop when I notice a few kids who continue to be flustered or dependent on me. I think that a minilesson went well only to see kids struggling with the idea during independent reading time. I want students to be able to practice new skills and strategies on their own, but when they can't I am tempted to swoop in to help so that they aren't sitting there confused. What else is there to do? After twenty-nine years of teaching, this is still tricky for me.

Scaffolding is complex, and Maggie and Kate help us to see how much of new learning we ask our students to hold onto without always giving them the tools to do so. Then they share the power of tools that they've used in classrooms. These tools include teaching charts, demonstration notebooks, micro-progressions, and bookmarks. Each one supports students in different ways, but they all help children work at higher levels.

The authors take complicated ideas for scaffolding and break them down so they can be readily used in classrooms. Maggie and Kate show how to align tools with individual student needs. Building on formative assessments, they show us how to use what we know about students to help them move to the next place. This book is not about ready-made tools, but rather about designing tools for and with students that will help them grow as readers and writers. The book goes beyond single skills or strategies. Instead, the focus is on practical ways to empower students and create independence.

The ideas are sophisticated, but Kate and Maggie make teachers feel like "we can do this!" The tips and tricks that they share are ones they have learned in real classrooms with real children in the midst of literacy workshops.

DIY Literacy: Teaching Tools for Differentiation, Rigor, and Independence is my favorite kind of professional book. Maggie and Kate trust that teachers have the key structures in place for literacy growth. They wrote a book that caused me to reflect on my own teaching and to think more deeply about scaffolding, rigor, and independence. But they did more than just get me thinking. They actually gave me concrete ideas and examples of how to work in more intentional ways with my students. Just as those experts on home improvement shows can transform a room in just a few days, Kate and Maggie have given us the wonderful gift of tools to transform our classrooms.

—*Franki Sibberson*

Acknowledgments

We would first like to acknowledge you, reader, and your hard work. We have never seen educators work harder. This inspired us, made our hearts ache to make things easier, and has been one of the primary motivations for this book. Thank you.

It is true that educational books stand on the shoulders of other texts, teachers, and curriculums, and this book may especially do so. Whether it is Marjorie Martinelli and Kristi Mraz's groundbreaking work on using teaching charts with the primary grades, or Lucy Calkins and the Reading and Writing Project's latest work on learning progressions, or the myriad talented teachers with whom we work and their exceptional ways of adapting curriculum and finding creative ways to help kids learn. Thank you to all who have come before us. We could not have done this without you.

Lucy Calkins helped to make this book a reality, both in suggesting it should exist and through her support as a mentor, a leader, and a teacher. Lucy is always able to see far beyond what we can see in ourselves. Thank you for believing. Thank you for your teaching.

We have been lucky to work in some of the best classrooms in the country. Deep gratitude goes to Leigh Anne Eck, our first brave Twitter contributor; Anne Good for jumping in with eagerness and verve; Brianna Friedman Parlitsis, for bringing primary charm to the pages of this upper-grade book; Sarah Reedy, for being our constant ally, contributor, and friend; Heather Burns, who has taken our work and carried it far down the road; Lindsey Aikman, for giving such a gift of time and energy in the middle of the busiest time of year; Elayne Lipkin, for her creativity, care, and stunning penmanship; Jess Lifshitz, for generously sharing her digital work; Kristen Warren, for her thoughtful and profound applications at every turn; Anna Bennett, for her sense of humor, heartfelt teaching, and delicious baked goods; Brandi Brown, for sharing such love and respect with her students and colleagues; and finally, Theresa Walter, for her willingness to jump in and try anything, and the stunning results she usually gets. These educators fuel not only our work but also our spirits. How can we get lost in the dark times when these teachers lead the way with such light and love?

We are fused with a learning community that influences us more than we can say. The Reading and Writing Project has truly shaped us into the educators we are today. Our colleagues are generous and thoughtful, and the thinking that alchemizes among them is transformational. Thank you in particular to Brooke Geller, who helped launch demonstration notebooks and co-created them with us over the years; to Colleen Cruz for being our staunchest and most brilliant ally; to Audra Robb and the entire middle-school team—past and present—whose companionship, brilliance, and wit heal us from week to week. To Marjorie Martinelli and Kristi Mraz for giving us their support in carrying the torch of teaching tools to the upper grades. And to Mary Ehrenworth, who has been our champion and our muse for so long now that thanks seem hardly enough—she has been a fuel cell to our work and to this book in particular.

Working with a good publishing company feels like growing up in a good home. We are proud to be a part of the Heinemann family, and we thank you for your support. To our editor, Tobey Antao, we thank you. We are delighted and stunned at how deftly you honed the work in ways that left us feeling empowered and excited. You take credit for nothing, but deserve so much. Eric Chalek, mostly we want to thank you for threading *Star Wars* references throughout our emails, but we suppose we could also thank you for the out-of-nowhere genius in the directions you helped us take this book. Monica Crigler, thank you not only for the design that makes our heart leap with pride, that makes us thrilled to tweet photos of the book, but also for the joyful, artistic spirit with which you do everything. Elizabeth Valway and Sarah Fournier, thank you for jumping in and making this happen. You were our deus ex machina, our knights in shining armor. Finally, we would like to thank Vicki Boyd, Lisa Fowler, and Patty Adams. Thank you for continuing to build a space for educators who love and believe in kids, teachers, and schools.

Our friends have been the wind at our back throughout this process, pushing us along with cheers and motivation, carrying us when we've stumbled. Nadine Baldasare, you have always been there to feed us, make us laugh, and anchor us in rough seas. Christopher "Jeans" Lehman, you are a treasure, not just to the world of education, but to our family. You are so very dear to us—thank you for your friendship and for your heart. Jen Serravallo, thank you for your steely support and professional brilliance. Donalyn Miller, Penny Kittle, and Franki Sibberson, thank you for your inspiration.

To Tara Brown, our son's caregiver: Without you we would never have been able to carve out the space to write this book. It is a gift to feel completely comfortable leaving your child in the care of someone else. Thank you for how wonderful you are with our boy. We thank our parents for their cheerleading and unwavering support. Also, thanks to Leah and Kristina for coming through in a pinch.

Finally, though he can't read this yet, we would like to thank our son, Bo. No matter what is going on, all we have to do is look into your eyes to know who we are again. You are our greatest joy. We write this book for you in hopes that your time in school is as deep and happy as you are right now.

Chapter One

Extending Our Reach

A few days ago, the taillight on our car went out. Our first thought was, "Oh jeez, there goes another 150 bucks," and we planned to take the car to our mechanic. Then we thought, "Why not do it ourselves? We are strong and capable people. We can do this." So we did what any modern, would-be car mechanic would do—we went to YouTube and watched videos. Emboldened by the power of the Internet, we marched out to our car with our tiny, we-live-in-the-city toolbox and confronted the busted taillight.

And we failed.

We didn't really know what to do. We didn't have the right tools to do the job, and we barely knew how to use the tools we did have. For a moment, we resigned ourselves to the large amounts of money we were going to have to pay someone to do it for us. But then we thought to find a teacher. We thought to ask Rich, Maggie's stepfather, if he could help us to fix the car ourselves.

"Well, that depends," he said. And he opened his truck of tools. You see, Rich travels with his truck stocked with every tool he could possibly need, and luckily we were traveling with him this day. He looked at our car, assessed the situation, and then taught us how to change a taillight for a whopping $3.67. What it took for us to save some serious money? A ratchet, a lightbulb, and someone to teach us.

Without those tools and the knowledge of how to use them, we couldn't "do it ourselves." We could assess what was wrong, we could get a sense of the steps from a YouTube video. But without the right tools, we could never have done the work effectively on our own. Without the right tools, and the knowledge of how to use them, our "Do It Yourself" dreams were out of reach.

In our teaching, we have faced impossible moments, those times when our inner teacher voice says, "It can't be done!" Maybe it was that kid we couldn't seem to reach—the one for whom we had tried everything we knew on our own to help but had yet to turn the corner. Or maybe it was a moment after a unit when, even though the unit seemed to go okay, we were depleted and unable to muster great energy for the next unit beginning the following day. "There has to be something to make this easier," we thought.

Of course, teaching children is never as simple as installing a taillight. However, we have often craved—in our work with students, teachers, and districts—the "truck full of tools" that could help us to do more of the work ourselves, or to make the work more effective (and a little easier) along the way. Alongside this, we have wished for the tools that could help our kids feel more like DIY warriors of their own learning. We have wanted tools that could help students work harder, smarter, and on their own.

Teachers have always used teaching tools in the classroom. To transfer information, we went from slates and chalk to carbon copies to anchor charts and interactive whiteboards and, now, the cloud. The tools we use in the classroom have changed, partly because our technology has advanced. But tools also evolve based on needs we uncover and dreams we begin to dream. Rethinking tools and their uses helps address what might appear to be insurmountable challenges. Because, in those tough "it's not working" situations, we know deep down that when our kids aren't engaged, or learning, or growing, there is something they are not getting from us that they need.

In this book, we strive to help you find, and teach your students to use, the right teaching tool for the job.

After all, we do what we do for the kids. The tool is there to help students do more, better work *on their own*. So we must always ask ourselves, "Are the teaching tools I offer my kids really helping them to grow?"

The Right Tool for the Job

To find the right tool for the job of teaching, we must first identify what the obstacle to getting the job done *is* exactly. Often the biggest problem we face when teaching students is not the curriculum, or the politics of education, or the lesson plan we have written. Most of the time the biggest problem we face is tougher than that; it's sneakier and harder to define. In this book, we tackle three such problems:

Memory: Our students are being taught so much, and so quickly, that they struggle to remember what they "should" know or do.

Rigor: Our students are not always doing the heavy lifting in class. When our students don't work hard, we know they are not getting all they can from school.

Differentiation: We struggle to meet the needs of all our students, and we sense that there are groups of kids who are not being inspired, pushed, or helped the way they need and deserve.

These real struggles get in the way of learning. True learning happens when students get the instruction that fits their needs, have the agency and motivation to work hard, and remember and recycle what they've learned. Sometimes we—teachers and kids—need teaching tools to help us to reach these goals. This is just the way of things; tools have *always* helped us reach farther than our bodies and minds allow us to alone. We have *always* needed a little bit of help to get to where we want to go. From the days of our earliest ancestors, human beings have relied on invented tools. (Just consider a stone axe, the wheel, duct tape, a pencil.) As educators and students, we are no different. Sometimes we can reach our dreams; we just need some help to do it.

There are many types of teaching tools to adopt and adapt to meet the needs of students. Chapter Two introduces and outlines a few—some of our favorites—and Chapter Six explores ways to make teaching tools effective and manageable. The tools we highlight include those shown in Figure 1–1 (see page 4). (Chapter Two provides a lengthier discussion of the examples shown in the figure.)

While we hope to empower you to make some useful teaching tools with your students, we spend the bulk of this book addressing not just *what* tools to use, but *how* these tools can help address specific challenges you face in your classroom. Chapter Three examines how teaching tools help students remember what has been taught before. Chapter Four dives into the work of using teaching tools to help students work with rigor, and Chapter Five offers ideas for how teaching tools help differentiate your teaching to match your students' needs. We have also included a "bonus chapter" that helps you to find the content that goes *on* all these teaching tools—the strategies, lessons, and tips that can help your students become the readers and writers they dream of becoming.

We are able to shift currents in our teaching when we step back, reflect upon the root issue for a student, group of students, or class, and offer a concrete, practical, visual tool to help address that bigger problem. After all, being frustrated when a child is refusing to clean her room rarely helps, nor does nagging. Instead, a star chart—a simple chart hung on the refrigerator marked with fun and flashy star stickers so your child can see all the times he or she made a smart choice—often does the trick.

Teaching tools can be the star charts of your classroom, the seemingly simple things that cause great positive change.

How Teaching Tools Help

The tools in our lives *improve* our lives. They save us energy, time, and struggle. Our son uses a little toy grocery cart to help him practice what he most wants to do right now but can't quite do on his own—walk. This tool helps him achieve his goal faster by allowing him to practice independently. Tools make the work easier, more manageable, and less stressful. They *help*.

Teaching tools help kids work hard and do better, sure. But they also help kids meet and match our deepest hopes for them. We hope they need us less, not more. We hope they become flexible problem solvers and are engaged in school and beyond. We hope that our kids become more powerful, independent readers and writers of a variety of texts. We crave these results as we teach, and yet often we get trapped in the hamster wheel of breadth—of being sure we have gotten to everything—rather than centering our work on depth. Teaching tools can clearly illustrate steps for exploration and growth toward these ends, and in doing so they can help make our hopes for our kids *their hopes for themselves*.

REPERTOIRE OR PROCESS CHARTS

Lists of strategies or steps hung in the classroom, often created and introduced with kids in whole-class teaching and referred to in conferences and small groups

I can think about a
CHARACTER's

Actions
Dialogue
Relationships
Choices
Problems

...and what these things tell me about the kind of person they are.

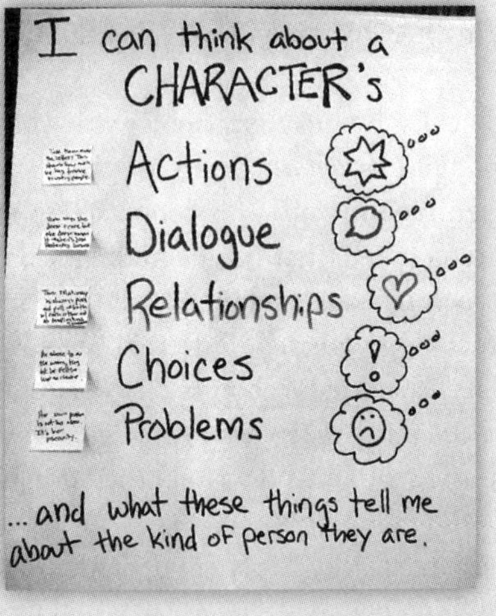

DEMONSTRATION NOTEBOOKS

Collections of teaching texts primarily for conferences and small groups

Doris is brave because she stands up for herself. For example, at the dinner table she brings up the dog to her parents and even argues a little with them even though she is scared.

Prompts to help
ANALYZE EVIDENCE

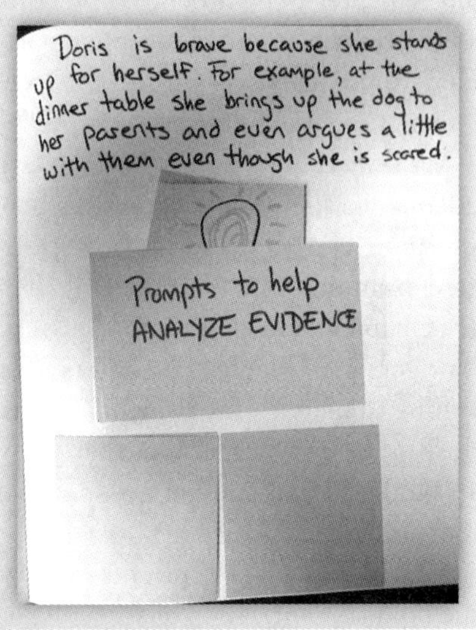

MICRO-PROGRESSIONS OF SKILLS

An agreed-upon range of levels for a particular skill, created and introduced in whole-class teaching and referred to in conferences and small groups

Jaz hit the field hockey ball with her stick and ran down the field. The sun was shining bright.

Jaz looked for someone to pass to, but her teammates all looked the other way. She hit the ball up the field and ran. The sun beat down hot on her face.

Jaz had the ball, and looked to her left to pass. Her teammates looked the other way. "Just ignore them," Jaz thought, but she shielded as she hit the ball up the field and ran. She felt her cheeks turn red.

• The scene shows what is happening in the moment.

• The scene includes setting details.

• The scene hints at the problem or emotions within the story.

• The details of the story are chosen because they reveal emotion.

• The scene includes the inner thinking of the character.

• The scene hints at the larger meaning, the character flaws, or the change in the story.

Improving Narrative Scenes

★   ★★   ★★★

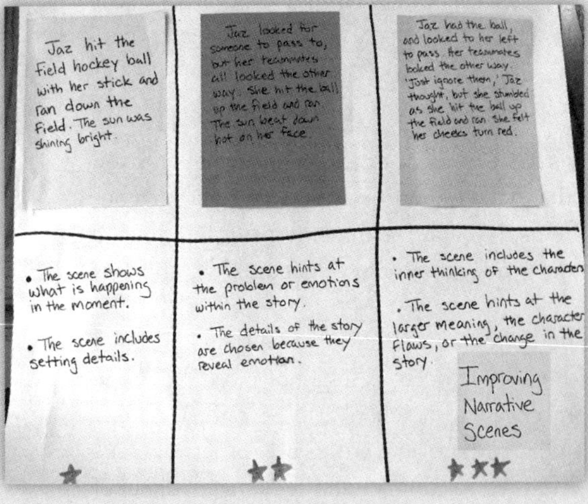

BOOKMARKS

Personalized lists of helpful strategies, tips, and lessons that kids make with a teacher's guidance

How many pages can I get to?
#

What kind of book should I read next?
☐ same character?
☐ Same theme?
☐ Same author?
☐ same genre?

Who can I talk to about this book?

How can I push my thinking about the CHARACTERS?
☐ Compare them?
☐ Focus on complexity?
☐ Look for little details

How can I push my thinking about the THEME?
☐ Start early in book
☐ Track theme ideas as I read

What online community can I find/form to discuss the book?

Figure 1–1 Examples of Teaching Tools

Teaching tools will not be the answer to every problem you face in your classroom, nor will they all by themselves create rigor and independence just by being in your students' hands. You will also need good teaching practices, a strong curriculum, and solid relationships with your kids. But we do argue that teaching tools are powerful assistants along the way.

We Use Teaching Tools to Make Teaching Clear

As literacy consultants at the Reading and Writing Project, we have been nurtured in a methodology of teaching that is always in search of the answer to the question, "But how do readers and writers actually *do* that?" We believe that one of our jobs as teachers is to demystify the very abstract world of what it means to be a reader or a writer. It is not enough for most students if we simply say, "When you read you should be thinking about the bigger meaning of the text." When we have taught in this way, we have felt deeply the unspoken question that follows: "But *how?*"

The way we demystify this work—the way we find the how—is to crack open the hood and look inside at the inner workings of reading and writing. We pause as we read and ask, "What am I doing here to make meaning?" And then we strive to put that work in generalizable, kid-friendly language so that we can charge into our classrooms with the good news: "Hey kids, I figured it out! Here is one way we can be better readers today." (For more on generating strategies like this, refer to the bonus chapter.)

We believe that one of the most effective ways to spur growth is to offer students clear steps and moves to try interesting, rigorous work in their reading and writing. In fact, we believe (and have learned from edu-heroes like Calkins, Anderson, Keene, Beers, and Bomer) that entire units can be crafted around a sequence of these steps and moves, also known as strategies. That is one way to make our teaching clear and to be sure that kids understand exactly how to do the things that they want to do. But as anyone steeped in strategy instruction can tell you, pretty soon you start to accumulate, well . . . an awful lot of strategies. Each day, whether in your whole-class lesson or in small-group lessons and conferences, the strategies come spilling out: "Good readers do this . . ." and "Writers of essays try to. . . ." Before long it begins to feel like an embarrassment of riches where students are swimming in tons of possible strategies. It is important to create authentic, deeply known repertoires of strategies for students, but sometimes these clear strategies become muddy from overcrowding.

Teaching tools help organize and bring clarity to the strategies in your classroom. A series of lessons on how to find the main idea in a text may demystify that skill for your students for the time that you are explicitly teaching it. However, a chart or a bookmark that keeps those strategies front and center, *and* allows your students to refer to and choose what will work best for them, gives students not just an understanding of the skill but a flight plan they can refer to whenever they are feeling off course.

We Use Teaching Tools to Bring Big Ideas and Goals to Life

Stay in education long enough and you will experience a sea change. A new idea or set of ideas will hit the educational landscape and suddenly professional development sessions, curriculum, and criteria will spring forth to address the next big thing. Perhaps it will be a standard, or a skill, or a desired quality that students should have. And the thing is, it will most likely be a really good idea. You will agree with it. It will excite you. But when you try to make that idea work in your classroom for your students, you might find it difficult to make the abstract come to life. For any worthwhile goal to be within arm's reach, many students need a boost. It helps to have a clear path of steps to follow when walking toward something new. One way to extend students' reach as they strive to meet a goal is to find a tool that can help.

Let's take one recent big idea in education as an example. John Hattie has performed comprehensive and helpful research around this question: "What has the biggest effect on learning in education?" In his book *Visible Learning* (2009), Hattie scours eight hundred meta-studies to look for the interventions, methods, and circumstances that have the largest effect on the growth and learning of students. His list is long, but it's what is at the top that compels. Figure 1–2 shows some of the primary influences on learning, among the top ten, according to Hattie.

Self-Reporting Grades: How well do students predict they will do? To what extent do students have expectations for their own learning?

Piagetian Programs: Does the teaching developmentally match the students in the room?

Formative Evaluation: Is the teacher assessing how students are doing before and during the unit, and adjusting teaching accordingly?

Figure 1–2 Some Top Influences on Learning, According to John Hattie

And here is the thing: This is a *really* good list. Hattie's research might just be some of the best, most research-based thinking out there (we think it is). The keys to successful learning and growth are empowering students to self-monitor their learning, meeting students where they are when teaching something new, and bookending units of study with *before* and *after* snapshots of student work so that growth (or lack thereof) is clear to see.

We have traced the lines from this research into classrooms, studying the intersection of what the research says and the practical nature of the everyday in schools. This is the place where we need to live and think as teachers—where the rubber meets the road. What does the research say about best practice *and* what does that look like at 8 a.m. on a Monday morning in a fifth-grade classroom in Brooklyn?

We might be tempted to simply weave bits of his suggestions into our daily practice, asking students to predict their success with a partner, maybe, or using formative evaluation here and there. But will we feel the full effect of that work if it's piecemeal? As we all know, a certain chemistry exists between research practices and practical application— sometimes it can fizzle, sometimes it can spark. Rather than relying on small, behind-the-scenes shifts that might not even be noticeable to students, we put this work in the kids' hands, perhaps by using a micro-progression, which gives students concrete ways to track their own progress. In this case, a micro-progression not only helps name the work we're doing with students but also shows it developing across time. More powerfully, and to Hattie's point, this teaching tool helps students embed the idea of constant self-assessment and progress into their own academic identities. Showing work via a micro-progression, or another teaching tool, is deeply rooted in practicality and the everyday, but the branches of this work reach toward the sky of big ideas and goals for kids.

We Use Teaching Tools to Help Learning Stick

Most of us, if asked why we wanted to teach, wouldn't say, "I really wanted to write curriculum and assess student work." Instead, we bet most would say we wanted to become teachers because we wanted to make a difference. We wanted to have an impact on students' learning and their lives. Yet, most of us have also faced moments of doubt. Instead of having the *Oh Captain! My Captain!* moments from the movies we so hoped to have when entering the profession, we at times feel more like the economics teacher from *Ferris Bueller's Day Off*, waiting for someone in the class to answer a question, asking forlornly, "Anyone? . . . Anyone?" These doubts make us question: Is our teaching making an impact? Are we making a difference?

Teaching tools create an impact on students' learning because they help students hold onto our teaching and become changed by the work in the classroom. They help teaching become "sticky," as Shanna Schwartz describes in *A Quick Guide to Making Your Teaching Stick, K–5* (2008). As Schwartz reminds us, rare is the child who can learn a new skill in one try. Instead, "one of our jobs as teachers is to provide the numerous iterations needed for a lesson to stick, thus helping children move through the approximation period into solid comprehension and use of a new concept" (1). Without this "solid comprehension" in our teaching, we can start to feel a sense of hopelessness and futility. Why work so hard on a unit, a lesson, or a stack of papers if we don't see a lasting effect?

There are three main reasons why teaching tools help teaching become stickier:

1. **They are visual.** We all have a drive and need to see things clearly. No matter the age, it helps to see things represented, spelled out, and broken down. In fact, a large portion of our brain tissues' sole job is to analyze images (Gazzaniga 2009). Visuals help us to understand and remember information. For example, we most likely do not recall the daily recommended servings of every food group, but the teeny tiny triangle at the top of the food guide pyramid is a clear (and sad) reminder that the total number of sweets we eat should be but a fraction of our total diet. In the same way, students can easily visualize

the difference between levels of work when they see them side-by-side on a micro-progression, and they can retain strategies better when they have a few easy icons on a bookmark or chart to prompt them.

2. **They make the abstract concrete.** We have all had the experience of trying to explain something complex to our students only to find ourselves caught in a "word salad," a confusing jumble of language that refuses to take shape. It's hard to clearly explain a tough concept or complex skill. Making a teaching tool—a demonstration notebook page, a micro-progression of skills—requires us to find the exact language to describe something abstract, like finding the main idea of a text or developing a thesis statement. It helps us corral our teaching by figuring out how to explain something big in a small amount of very clear words. This clarity helps teaching stick.

3. **They encourage repeated practice.** Think of a time you learned something new, perhaps a new language, a new sport, or a new recipe. Chances are you practiced that thing a number of times. The number of times practiced is different from person to person, although there are statistics. A quick Internet search will show that one has to practice something for twenty-one days in order to make it a habit. Psychologist Jeremy Dean (2013), in his book *Making Habits, Breaking Habits: Why We Do Things, Why We Don't, and How to Make Any Change Stick*, points out that twenty-one days is only enough time to make a habit out of something easy or small, like drinking a glass of water in the morning before a cup of coffee. Anything more complex—say, learning how to determine a theme of a poem—could take much longer. These tougher habits took, on average, around 254 days of daily practice to solidify, or the better part of a year! When turning strategies into habits and lessons into daily practice, teaching tools can remind kids to practice and practice often, just like the *Drink more water* reminder on the fridge.

Reaching Our Goals, Reaching Our Dreams

So far we have outlined how teaching tools help address some of the root issues with learning in our classrooms. And it is true that teaching tools are invaluable when meeting a *need* you have in your teaching. But they also help you achieve your teaching *dreams*. Dreams of helping students work hard. Dreams of helping kids have more of *those* moments, the ones where they get it. Dreams of students feeling seen—by us and by each other.

As literacy consultants, we have never seen teachers work harder than we do now. And we have watched teaching tools help them feel as though all of their hard work is worth it. In part, the tools help get traction going with teaching and learning. In larger part, the tools inspire kids to work as hard as we are. These tangible, colorful, personalized offerings of our teaching are individual gifts to students. They communicate the message of *I see you. I see your next steps. Let me help you. Here is this.* These teaching tools invite kids in on the work of the class in a way that is tailored to them, allowing students to take control of their learning and do it themselves.

When we take on DIY projects, from remodeling a bathroom to making a new teaching chart, we know that part of the joy in this project is going to come from our own efforts. And while many times the hallmark of a DIY project is its imperfections, these flaws often become marks of character, points of pride, and evidence of learning.

One key to experiencing joy is working hard and seeing that hard work pay off. When mathematicians solve a problem they've been grappling with for months, when a musician perfects a performance of a complicated piece, when a learner masters a difficult concept, joy arrives.

It is our greatest hope that the tools we offer here will help your students to work hard, to hold onto what they know, and to see themselves in the curriculum you teach.

Onward to joy!

Chapter Two

An Introduction to Teaching Tools

You are never strong enough that you don't need help.
—César Chávez

Types of Teaching Tools

Picture yourself on a road trip. You have your delightfully unhealthy snacks, your music, your traveling companion, the open road. You also have your maps. Depending on who you are and the way your mind works, your map takes on different forms. If you are Kate, you have a GPS yelling directions at you every minute. If you are Maggie, you have an old-school atlas. If you are Kate's mom, you have a list of handwritten directions by your side. The result is the same—you arrive at your destination. Every journey includes the need to solve problems, like taking a wrong turn and needing your map to get you back on course. But, depending on the type of person you are and what the situation requires, one kind of map will work better for you than another. Whether it's the quality of your memory or your spatial awareness, the type of map matters.

There are, of course, many journeys we take in our classrooms throughout a school year. Like on any worthy trip, it will help to have some maps—in this case what we call "teaching tools"—guiding your teaching and your students' learning, helping everyone solve the inevitable wrong turns and dead ends that arise. Because, chances are, you have looked out at your students at times and felt they have looked like lost travelers, some searching for help at every turn and others wandering off into the hills. Teaching tools help teach students the way, so that someday they will know the way on their own, like the road home.

The type of tools we use in our classroom matters, just as much as travelers having the right map for a trip. Students need similar options for choosing the best teaching tools to support their learning. Creating a variety of teaching tools to help students navigate their learning allows opportunities for choice and autonomy, putting the decision making into their hands.

What follows is a quick guide to the four central teaching tools discussed in this book. For each, we provide a quick description of the tool, its central purpose, a step-by-step guide for making the tool, and an annotated example or two. We hope it gives you a place to start when designing helpful and effective tools, or offers inspiration as you find ways to make them your own.

Teaching Charts: Teaching into Repertoire and Process

Teaching charts are helpful teaching tools when students would know *how* to work if they could just have a list of *what* to do.

A teaching chart, as shown in Figure 2–1, is a list of steps or strategies that students can use to help them in their work. There are many ways to talk about charts in our 3–8 classrooms, as well as different types of charts we can make and use in our teaching.

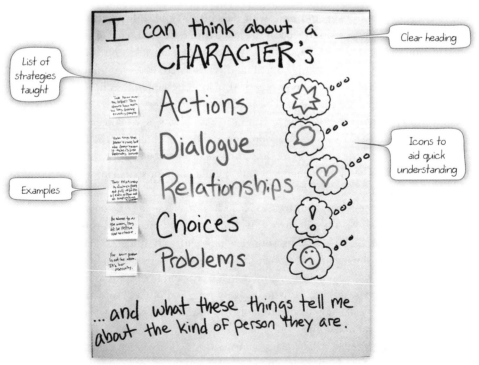

Figure 2-1 Example of a Repertoire Teaching Chart

As our colleagues and friends Kristi Mraz and Marjorie Martinelli describe deftly in *Smarter Charts K–2: Optimizing an Instructional Staple to Create Independent Readers and Writers* (2012) and *Smarter Charts for Math, Science, and Social Studies: Making Learning Visible in the Content Areas* (2014), **a repertoire chart** records a list of strategies that help students work toward a big skill, say, all of the ways (*strategies*) a reader can analyze a character (*skill*) while they read (see Figure 2–1). **A process chart**, on the other hand, takes a big skill, like determining the theme of a text, and breaks it down into the steps students would take to perform that skill, as shown in Figure 2–2. (*First, name the problem in the story. Next, put that problem into one word or phrase. Finally, think about what the text is teaching you about that word or phrase.*) Both types of charts are lists to help students get going or keep going in their work, largely by recording the teaching that has already taken place, preventing its loss in the sands of time.

The best charts, whichever the type, are those made in front of students and as collaboratively as possible. Often teachers draw on student talk to gather the information that they put on a chart or create opportunities for students to make models that go alongside each step or strategy.

Repertoire and process teaching charts make clear to students the instructional choices they have at any given time. They help students get to work and keep working with greater independence.

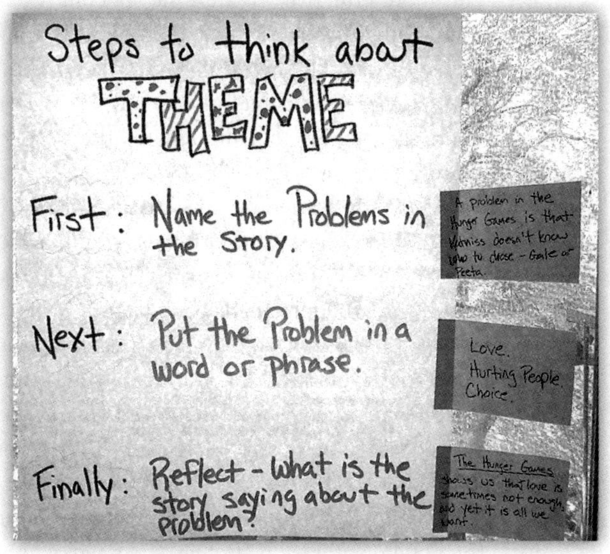

Figure 2-2 Example of a Process Chart

How to Make a Teaching Chart

STEP ONE: Ask yourself, "What skill (or content) am I centering this chart around?" This will be your HEADING. It could be as simple as "Ways to Think About Characters," as complex as "Comparisons We Can Make Across Books," or as habit-based as "How to Keep Writing When I Feel Done."

STEP TWO: List the strategies, ways, or steps necessary to accomplish that skill underneath the heading, preferably in colorful, clear writing. This will become the menu, or list. The more kid-friendly, icon-rich you make your menus, the better. (See Chapter Six for more ways to make your charts visually compelling and useful.)

STEP THREE: Hang your chart in a place where your students can access it easily. As they say, location, location, location! Your students shouldn't have to crane their necks to use a chart or wonder where to look. (See Chapter Six for more ways to organize your charts in your classroom.)

Demonstration Notebooks: Showing Students the *How*

Demonstration is helpful when learning something new. Whether it be how to Zumba, how to swaddle a baby, or how to write a poem, demonstration makes learning easier and more effective. "Watch me" becomes an incredibly powerful phrase that we speak as teachers. We know this. "Watch me as I notice what the author is doing as a writer in this scene" we say, and then we reflect on how Kate DiCamillo uses the colors of yellow and orange—the colors of fire—in *The Tiger Rising*. This demonstration is the in-the-moment teaching that illuminates the work for students before they are asked to try it themselves.

A demonstration notebook is a collection of interactive lessons the teacher can use to demonstrate repeatedly with kids, whether individually in conferences or in small groups across the day, unit, and year. It is a notebook full of the lessons and strategies that you know your students need. Each page identifies a need you've seen in your students, offers a clear solution or strategy, and creates space (most often in the form of a blank sticky note) to demonstrate and work with the strategy in real time with kids.

Demonstration notebooks aren't made overnight: it takes a bit of thoughtful listening and consideration as to what your kids need to identify the strategies you'll put in your notebook. You'll need to consider what lessons you find yourself returning to again and again and what strategies your kids need the most. But then, once you've made a page in the notebook for each strategy you need, you have a go-to guide that's ready whenever you need a quick lesson, the minute you need it, for a long time to come. In a way, demonstration notebooks contain a collection of extreme makeovers. That is, they curate examples of work that explicitly show vast improvement (and clearly name the moves to make that improvement happen). Because this collection of demonstrations is housed inside a notebook, it is portable and easy to use when gathering small groups of students.

Just imagine: Your class is working on literary essays and you walk around, looking over their shoulders to see how things are going. All of a sudden you notice that a few of your students are struggling to analyze the evidence they have selected for their essays. Instead of wringing hands, or waiting for the revision portion of the unit, or telling them, "Hey, you should really analyze your evidence—just, you know, analyze it!" you gather the kids you see struggling to analyze evidence from a text. You open up the demonstration notebook to a page on analyzing evidence that you created earlier (see Figure 2–3) and demonstrate ways to analyze evidence using the prompts on the elaboration cards you made. Then, you show students how to put those prompts to work by using the blank

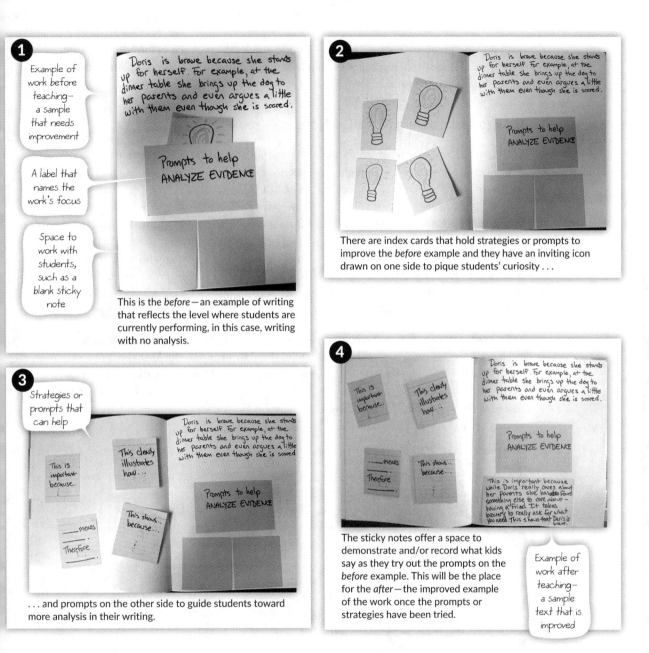

Figure 2–3 Demonstration Notebook Page

sticky note to rewrite the sample text that needs improvement. This way, you show students how to use the elaboration cards by quickly modeling your own use of them, thereby improving the quality of the *before* sample text in front of them. Then, for good measure, you let them pick an elaboration card to try their hand at it, perhaps with a partner right there in the small group or aloud on their own during a conference. This way, they get a little supported practice before they work on their own. Demonstration notebooks help kids to practice a skill in the company of others before having to do it on their own.

How to Make a Demonstration Notebook

STEP ONE: Identify the teaching that a group of students need around a certain reading or writing skill. For example, you might have notes on some students that say "having trouble with verb tense" or "inferences feel low level." Leaning on a piece you are writing with your kids, or a read-aloud text your class knows, write an example that shows this problem in action. In other words, write like them for a few lines at the top of the demonstration notebook page. This is the "before" example. For instance, you might write, "Adam goes to the kitchen and said," as an example for the students struggling with verb tense, or "She is sad," for older kids making lower-level inferences. You might even want to create a label that brands the page with the work you're focusing on, such as "Tackling Tricky Verb Tense" or "Aim for Sky-High Inferences."

STEP TWO: Choose one to three strategies or a few prompts or tips that could help the students do better and improve their work. Find these strategies by thinking about the *what* and the *how*—*what* does the writer or reader need to do and *how* might they go about doing that? (See the bonus chapter for ways to develop these strategies yourself and our favorite resources to consult.) Jot these strategies down in kid-friendly language underneath the

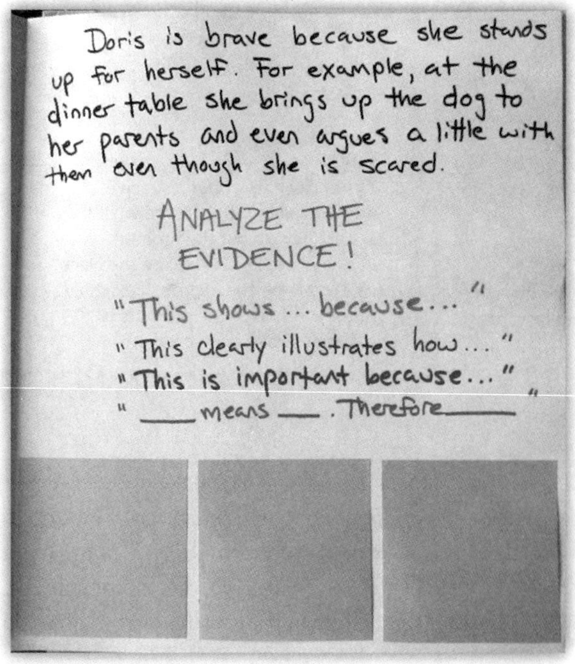

Figure 2-4 This demonstration notebook page shows the prompts listed on the page instead of on cards.

"before" writing. Use a different color marker if you list the strategies underneath the "before" writing (to view a color version of Figure 2–4, and the other figures in this book, refer to the "Companion Resources" section of the *DIY Literacy* page on www.Heinemann.com). Or, as in the sample shown in Figure 2–3, try putting each strategy on an index card that gets tucked into a pocket on the page. Graphics, artistry, or just a bit of color can make this space engaging for students (for more design tips, see Chapter Six).

STEP THREE: Create space for you to demonstrate by putting small stacks of blank sticky notes underneath the strategies. This is the space for the "after" example you will make with students. Choose the sticky note size by how much room you will need to write with your students. This is the space where you demonstrate how the strategy improves the "before" example or where you collaborate with students to improve it together.

Micro-progressions of Skills: Supporting and Clarifying Growth

Micro-progressions show the way toward higher levels of work. By providing actual examples of work that's improving, as well as listing the qualities that make up each "level" of work, micro-progressions allow for both self-assessment and self-assignment (see Figure 2–5).

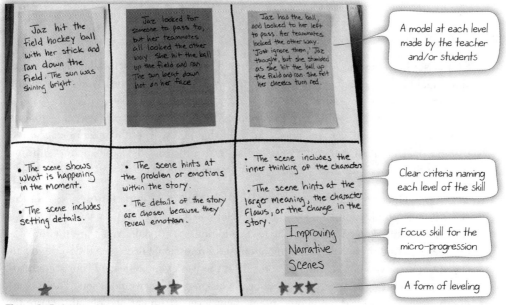

Figure 2–5 A Micro-progression for Narrative Writing

There are times when we observe a student working and we are met with an internal twist of anxiety, the gnawing sense that we aren't really sure what to say. Sometimes we are not positive what the *best* lesson is in a particular situation. We know we want the work to get "better," but what, exactly, does "better" mean?

Lucy Calkins and her colleagues at the Teachers College Reading and Writing Project have spearheaded the work of mapping out possible learning progressions for various skills and genres in reading and writing. In the books *Writing Pathways, Grades K–8* (Calkins 2015) and *Reading Pathways*, which is part of the Units of Study for Teaching Reading, Calkins argues that only by knowing the full trajectory of a certain skill can we possibly create a pathway for how to get there with students. The Reading and Writing Project has done transformative work using learning progressions to help teachers see how students' writing and reading can improve across grade levels. Micro-progressions work on a smaller scale, zooming in on a smaller span of a skill's levels (such as beginning, intermediate, and advanced) and pairing each level with short pieces of model text. These micro-progressions can be powerful tools for students to use directly as they guide their own learning. The small span of levels paired with the short pieces of model text show the subtle graduation—the small steps between levels of work. This helps students see exactly where they are and where they could go next on any reading or writing skill.

Micro-progressions of skills clearly show students the way to improve upon their work, but more importantly, they offer support for teachers to teach students how to assess *themselves*. "Take a look at your work," we say, "Where would you place it? Where are you?" Then micro-progressions allow students to set goals, using the next level to plan and envision their future work. A micro-progression creates a visible path for your class to follow as they lift the level of their work.

How to Make a Micro-progression

STEP ONE: Decide what skill will be developed by the micro-progression. The focused skill should be one of enough importance that your students will be asked to repeatedly perform it—either across the unit, the year, or the school day. This is largely because micro-progressions take some time to develop. Micro-progressions also take time to learn how to use, so you will want to choose the skills that kids will get the most mileage out of using. Consider labeling the micro-progression with the focused skill, such as "Improving the Quality of a Narrative Scene" or "Interpreting the Themes of Stories."

STEP TWO: Once you have determined a skill, develop the criteria for each level of that skill. That is, think about the skill as it develops in sophistication. What is the easiest rendition of this skill? What is the highest rendition of this skill? What are the levels in between? To find these levels, you might consult professional texts (see the Appendix for suggestions), or you could immerse yourself in the work you are asking your students to accomplish, putting yourself in their shoes by asking, "What would it look like to work at a high level here?" "What about an emergent level?" It might be helpful to write the examples first, and then step back to name what you did, thereby uncovering the criteria for each level. We have found it helpful to prepare this ahead of time so that you have a clear sense of where students are and what level they might be able to achieve.

STEP THREE: Work with your students to create models for each level, written above or below the written criteria on your micro-progression. This, naturally, works best if there is an existing class text or class topic being worked on. These demonstration models serve as concrete examples for students to hold onto as they work independently. Collaborative creation of these models allows students to feel a sense of ownership and agency over the tools they will then use independently—an essential ingredient for rigor. It can help to present one of the models already written, giving students an example and vision of the work. Once completed, hang up your micro-progression in a place where all of your students can see it (or make it accessible digitally) so that they may refer to the chart as they work.

Bookmarks: Creating Personalized Action Plans

Bookmarks allow students to personalize and keep close tabs on the work they are practicing in their reading or writing (see Figure 2–6 on page 20).

In the midst of a busy Saturday, you rush out of the house to begin a flurry of errands. There's not much time to focus and think through all that needs to be done. So you pause. You pull out a pen. You write a quick list of to-do's and reminders. A feeling of *I can do this* washes over you, replacing the original panic of the crunched day. The act of writing down each task and creating an efficient order is enough to create a sense of control and possibility.

Now picture your students. Every forty to fifty minutes or so they are asked to switch gears completely and focus on something different. (If they are in middle school, chances are they also have to traverse the tricky waters of the hallway in between.) Students are required to juggle quite a bit. It can help to pause within your curriculum and ask your kids which lessons, tips, and strategies have worked best for them. Allowing students to decide and write down for themselves the teaching that is most helpful creates space for them to be self-directed and reflective on the teaching happening in the classroom. These student-led bookmarks become powerful tools for growth.

Helping students to write down a personalized bookmark of strategies they want or need to remember can act as a helpful "grocery list" of tips. In *Getting Things Done*, David Allen (2001) argues that our brains can only hold so much without some organized assistance. In fact, research shows the physical act of writing activates the part of our brains that brings desired information to the forefront, triggering us to focus and set intention (Klauser 2001). Research also shows that people who write down their goals and share them with others are 33 percent more successful in accomplishing these goals.

We, as humans, need a way to list out *for ourselves* how we will accomplish a task or tackle tough work. Bookmarks can serve this purpose for our students, whether they

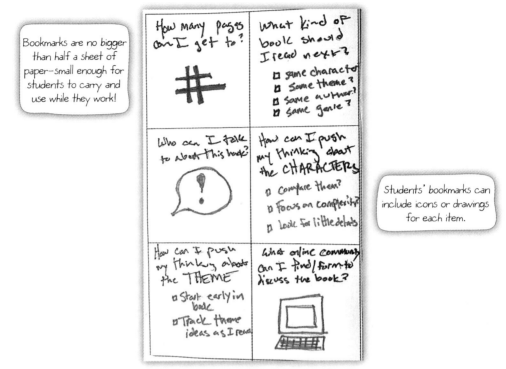

Figure 2–6 A Teacher's Model of a Bookmark

are trying to draft a report or get ready for a book club conversation. When students take inventory of things they've learned and write down goals and to-do's, they send themselves down a path of their own learning and are more likely to be successful.

How to Make a Bookmark

STEP ONE: Gather resources from your teaching and make sure they are accessible to students. Since students will be creating their bookmarks based on the lessons you have taught them, they will need to be able to see those lessons. Charts, micro-progressions, notebooks, and handouts should all be where the kids can get them. In addition, students will need paper that is cut to the size you think will be most handy (many times bookmarks are "bookmark" sized so they can be easily stuck in books and notebooks for easy access), pencils to draft their bookmarks, and pens and colored pencils to mark their final drafts. Certainly, kids could make their bookmarks digitally and store them on their devices.

STEP TWO: Demonstrate how you select what goes on your bookmark. Name a goal for your bookmark, such as "Ways to Write Descriptively" or "My Best Test-Taking Strategies." Show students how you decide which lessons, tips, steps, and strategies will help you best reach your goal. This quick demonstration helps students take stock of all they have learned, as well as choose lessons or strategies wisely to meet a goal.

STEP THREE: Offer support to students as they make their own bookmarks. As students work, they may need help making choices or remembering what worked for them and what didn't. Make sure each student has a partner they can talk to, confer with those who seem lost, and pull small groups of kids that can help each other as the kids work.

So Now What?

As anyone who has taken a road trip knows, the map is not the journey. The map is a support. Having a great teaching tool can be a support to kids in your classroom, but we have found that simply hanging a good-looking micro-progression is not enough to enact true change.

   The following chapters focus on how several key teaching tools—charts, demonstration notebooks, micro-progressions, and bookmarks—can address some common troubles that arise during teaching and learning: Chapter Three devotes itself to seeing how teaching tools can help students remember to use what you have already taught. Chapter Four looks at how to use tools to increase rigor. And Chapter Five examines how teaching tools can help differentiate your teaching to meet the variety of needs in your classroom.

   We hope that the work in this book can be as transformative for you as it has been for us, and for so many of the educators we work with. But the idea of *transforming* can be quite intimidating. So for now, let's remember that we are on a journey and that, in the words of Laozi, the ancient Chinese philosopher and poet, "a journey of a thousand miles begins with a single step."

✦ Bonus Chapter

How Do I Find (and Write) Strategies for Teaching Tools?

You've always had the power, my dear.
You had to learn it for yourself.
—Glinda, the Good Witch, *The Wizard of Oz*

Throughout this book, we focus on the teaching tools that can help all of your students become more independent, rigorous readers and writers. Specifically, we discuss how using these tools helps address some of the more pernicious issues that arise when we teach, issues around memory, rigor, and differentiation.

Perhaps, after reading the previous chapter, you leapt to action and ran to Staples to buy chart paper, markers, and large multicolored sticky notes. Then you ran home (we're not sure why in this image you are constantly running, but go with us for a moment . . .) and got right to work making a process chart to help your kids learn how to delve into the work of visualizing stories as they read. You wrote your title, "How to Visualize Scenes Like a Pro," in big, colorful letters and then, just as you were ready to write down the steps for envisioning deeply, you balked. A realization hit you—you don't actually know offhand the steps to visualizing a text in a way that leads to greater comprehension. What are they? Where do you find them?

We've been there. It's a humbling moment, this awareness that we don't have at our fingertips the content we most need to teach our kids—the steps, the tricks, the strategies they can reach for when they want to do more as readers or writers. This bonus chapter is dedicated to this moment. In the next few pages we'll discuss people and places to turn to when looking for strategies to make your own teaching tools. And, most importantly, we will help you turn inward to learn ways to build your own strategies from scratch.

We Need Strategies

When Maggie first started teaching, she knew just the tip of the iceberg when it came to the teaching of reading (or writing, for that matter). She knew, for example, that it helped if kids knew the things readers did in their minds as they read, and that modeling helped kids do that work more powerfully. She knew there were some big reading skills you could teach, like decoding, predicting, inferring, and so on. Maggie would sit down to prepare a text to be read aloud to her students, and she would try to model her thinking around a certain reading skill. It sounded a little like this:

> "So now watch as I infer as I read. (*Reads a little of the text.*) Okay, so what I'm inferring now is that this character is acting like she is brave with this guy, but really she is terrified of failure, probably because of the way her mom treats her and because of the fact that secretly, she loves him. See how I inferred? Okay, now you do it."

While Maggie's demonstration was good, for the students struggling to infer (or who didn't know what inferring meant), it felt like a magic trick. "Watch me as I do this thing you aren't sure how to do . . . *presto!* I did it! Now you do it. . . ."

What Maggie did not have in her teaching yet were the strategies, the tricks and tips and small steps that would help her students to progress along a certain skill. She knew the end point: "I want my kids to infer!" And she knew what that end point should look like, but the path to get to that destination stayed vague for her, and for her students, until she began to study up on strategies.

Thirty years ago, conversations converged on what it meant to teach kids to read and comprehend. This research began to uncover the cognitive processes that proficient readers use most often when reading, thinking, and discussing texts (Pearson et al. 1992). There was a new call that "reading teachers understand the cognitive processes used most frequently by proficient readers and that they provide explicit and in-depth instruction focused over a long period of time on these strategies" (Keene and Zimmermann 1997). Educators from across the field began weaving curricular stories around this research for both reading and writing instruction, introducing essential professional texts on what strategies to teach and, most importantly, *how* to teach them. In *Mosaic of Thought,* Ellin Keene and Susan Zimmermann offered ideas for strategies, including the essential work of using sensory images to enhance comprehension. Harvey and Goudvis wrote the groundbreaking *Strategies That Work* (2000). In the touchstone texts *The Art of Teaching Reading* (2001) and *The Art of Teaching Writing* (1986), Lucy Calkins taught how to craft minilessons around these strategies, not with a manual of lessons but from authentic "observations of readers." Most recently, in *The Reading Strategies Book* (2015), Jennifer Serravallo shares more than three hundred reading strategies, as step-by-step how-to's, for readers to meet thirteen different literacy goals.

The teaching tools in this book are connected to this ancestry. Throughout our decade working with Lucy Calkins and our colleagues at the Reading and Writing Project, we have been nurtured to be on constant lookout for specific strategies that could elevate the work of readers and writers. This led to a natural pairing of tools and strategies, a matchmaking of sorts between concrete teaching tools and practical reading or writing strategies. Each tool focuses on a skill students need (*what* they need to learn to do better) and strategies (*ways* to help students learn and perform that skill on their own). We've found that determining the skill of the teaching tool comes somewhat easier. Just think to yourself, "What does this child need right now?" The strategies? That can be a bit more complicated.

Here are our go-to resources to find the strategies you seek.

Bring in Backup: Three Ways to Find Help When You Need It

Robin. Chewbacca. Samwise Gamgee. We shine brighter with the help of our sidekicks. Sidekicks offer help when it is most needed. There will be times when you'll need help finding the right strategies. Often these times arise when you are making a teaching tool, forced to put pen to paper, calling forth what you know about the teaching of reading or writing. Chances are that you'll be running low on time, energy, or ideas in these moments (or perhaps a mixture of all three). You will need a sidekick.

In our work as literacy consultants, we cannot count the times that someone has asked us for the "cheat sheet of nonfiction reading strategies." What's great is, they exist! You just have to know where to look. Here are three ways to find a sidekick and bring in the curricular backup you need.

1. **Never teach alone.** It's strange how teaching can be so lonely. After all, we are surrounded by people every second of every day. But as the sole adult in the classroom, it is easy to get caught in the trap of closing our door and doing our thing. This can be liberating, as in, "Today I am going to close my door and teach poetry even though we are 'supposed' to be doing test prep, because my kids and I need some joy." But, if this is our general state of being, we can become isolated in both spirit and practice. Instead, we encourage educators to create communities of practice, inside or outside of their schools, so that they can learn from others and share their knowledge.

   We have been taught to center professional development around creating these kinds of communities. Whether it be by holding a lab site where teachers gather in one classroom together, practicing teaching methods like conferring with readers, or by meeting with grade-level teams to plan an upcoming unit, we believe only by working together can we can get better. As Meenoo Rami wisely writes in *Thrive: 5 Ways to (Re)Invigorate Your Teaching*, "an accomplished teacher must be connected. If we expect our students to be active, responsible and independent digital and global citizens we need to be models for them. If we are striving to create a system where the role of the teacher is no longer the lone expert in the room but a co-learner, we need to model that for our students, as well" (2014).

Having a trusted community of educators provides a place to go when trouble hits. We need professional friendships to get smarter and grow, but also to have a lifeline to email, text, or tweet on a Sunday night when we need three strategies for adding imagery to informational writing!

2. **Hit the books.** Another way to find strategies is to locate the right professional text. While having a community of actual people is important, you can find friends in the pages of books by educators who have published their ideas. Many times these texts will answer concrete questions, such as "How do I teach students to talk more deeply about their books?" while also offering a larger conversation around the structures, philosophies, or key concepts that contextualize the practices that support such work. In other words, professional books can be more than just repositories of strategies; they can become personal education professors. Here are a few professional texts that have rocked our world when trying to find strategies in a pinch (refer to the Appendix for more titles):

    Units of Study Series in Reading and Writing by Lucy Calkins and Colleagues from the Teachers College Reading and Writing Project

    These series are an essential resource for lessons (with all the bells and whistles of good teaching) for students in reading and writing, for grades K–8.

    Craft Lessons by Ralph Fletcher and JoAnn Portalupi

    In this classic text, Ralph and JoAnn offer core lessons that help students improve their writing, providing examples and description to help you on your way.

    The Reading Strategies Book by Jennifer Serravallo

    In this book Jen answers the call for an in-depth, organized, and easily accessible list of reading strategies across fiction and nonfiction, and across a range of reading levels and abilities.

    Energize Research Reading and Writing by Christopher Lehman

    In this book Chris illuminates practical strategies that can help teachers become more powerful research readers, note-takers, and writers.

3. **Go online.** For fun, try out an exercise with us: Pick something you would like your students to get better at doing (citing sources, summarizing, using strategies for critical reading). Now, go to your online search engine and type in

About 47,600,000 results (0.59 seconds)

Teaching Critical Reading | GSI Teaching & Resource Center
gsi.berkeley.edu/.../**critical-reading**-intr... ▾ University of California, Berkeley ▾
Students are assigned heavy **reading** lists throughout their years at UC Berkeley, and
frequently they skimp on their **reading**. On Berkeley's 2012 University of ...

Teaching Critical Reading - Brown University
https://www.brown.edu/.../**teaching**.../**teaching-critical-r**... ▾ Brown University ▾
How can I **teach** my **students to read critically**? ... **Teaching** Commons); **Teaching**
Critical Reading (from UC – Berkeley's Center for **Teaching** and Learning); Five ...

Teaching Critical Reading with Questioning Strategies - ASCD
www.ascd.org/.../... ▾ Association for Supervision and Curriculum Develop... ▾
And thank goodness; our world needs **students** who can **read** texts **critically**, not just ...
or try to detour the group from the **lesson** (What time does this period end?) ...

Strategies for Teaching Critical Reading
academic.pg.cc.md.us/~wpeirce/MCCCTR/crit**read**.html ▾
Strategies for **Teaching Critical Reading**. 1. Preview the ... Your **students** will not learn
to **read critically**--also a valuable skill in your discipline. Your passive ...

The Search Results for "Teach Students to Read Critically"

a searchable phrase, like "teach students to read critically." Hit Search. Boom. You are most likely looking at pages of possible lesson ideas. (You're welcome.)

Of course, the trouble with this solution is that you get EVERYTHING, the good, the bad, and the ugly. The Internet is a vast collection of seriously democratic posting. You can find yourself going down a time wormhole sifting through all of those hits to find the gold nugget. Here are a few tips to spot the gold when exploring online:

a. Check out the source. Is it respected? What's the background of the author? Is the source tied to an organization or affiliation? How well connected is the author? Does the author cite other sources or include links to similar sources?

b. Check out the date. Is the source current? Dated?

c. Check out the order. Is the source prioritized high on the list by the search engine? Or is it buried deep in the pages of the search?

d. Check out other sources. When you read across several resources, can you spot specific trends? Does the source fit inside the rest of the conversation about the topic? Does it make sense?

e. Check out the distractions or embellishments. Is there just a little too much clip art? Do the graphics overshadow the content? Is substance there, something to teach tomorrow when you scratch beneath the surface? Most importantly, does the content offered align with the goals your students have for themselves, and the goals you have for them?

To save time, it helps to know where to look. Many educators use sites like Pinterest to find communities of like-minded teachers that post lesson ideas, charts, and strategies. Others cultivate a Twitter community to follow respected colleagues, ask questions, and engage in chats to help expand their repertoire of teaching moves and ideas. Cast a wide net. Explore broadly. Find your community and tap into the digital resources the Internet offers.

Everybody needs a helping hand from time to time. Learning communities, whether they are online, published, or in person, are essential for our professional growth as educators. And it is also true that we shouldn't always need to look outside for the answers. Over time, if our only answer to the question "What can I teach my kids about XYZ?" is "Ask someone who knows more," our teaching self-esteem will suffer. Although asking for help is a good thing, knowing how to find the answers to our questions is often incredibly rewarding. This self-reliance, the ability to write our own lessons and create our own curriculum, is powerful. It allows us to respond to the kids in front of us, for our class to feel seen, and for students to continue to see us as an invaluable resource in the room.

What follows is a handful of concrete steps to use as a way to create reading and writing strategies from scratch and to pave your own way.

Do It Yourself: Mining Your Own Work for Strategies

Independence is powerful. For centuries, countries have fought for it, teenagers have rebelled for it, and hearts have yearned for it. This entire book is built on the hope that students will feel and employ greater independence throughout their academic lives.

And just as we all value independence for our students, we value it in our own lives as well. In our years co-writing curriculum with the Reading and Writing Project and working with teachers and students, we've been trained to generate our own strategies, to answer the question "How do I teach my kids to . . .?" ourselves. These self-made strategies come from an authentic source—our own reading and writing.

How to Write Strategies

Finding a strategy to teach students to read and write more powerfully is a little like learning how to get your first child to sleep through the night. You need the advice of experts, for sure, be it your mother, a book written by a respected PhD, or the guys down the street with five kids. You need the wisdom of those who have gone before you, and then you just need to figure out what weird thing works for you and your family. The same is true when we are trying to find the right strategies for our readers and writers. Outside sources are invaluable, as is diving in and doing the work ourselves. To write strategies, we have been taught to lean on what we do when we actually read and write. Here is one way to create a strategy.

First, think about WHAT you want to teach. Many times, the WHAT is the skill you want to teach. The WHAT is the thing you want your students to be able to do at the end of your teaching. Perhaps you want your readers to predict or summarize or interpret a symbol in a text. Or maybe you want your writers to generate some writing-about-reading entries in their notebooks, create more consistent paragraphs, or elaborate on evidence they have researched. The first step is figuring out what exactly you want to teach the students. It might sound like this:

> **THE WHAT** = Writers create paragraphs as they write stories.

Figuring out what you want to teach tends to come swiftly and easily. You probably already have strengths in seeing a particular thing kids need. Perhaps seeing grammatical needs comes easy to you, or structural needs like topic sentences. Or maybe paragraphing pops out at you first. Celebrate this strength of seeing! But be conscious of staying too close inside the parameters of what you see naturally. That is, you'll want to make sure to try to see a lot of different kinds of WHATs, or needs, that students have. If you are easily able to see convention issues, try looking for craft needs, and the like. By seeing a wide range of skills to teach, you'll up your chances to meet the needs of more students.

The chart on the next page shows some other examples of WHATs that can help keep your horizons broad when creating strategies.

Next, think about HOW students will accomplish that skill. This HOW is the strategy or the *way* students will perform the skill. For instance, *how* exactly does one interpret a symbol in a text? Or, what is the best *way* to write a thesis statement when writing an essay? Many times, this HOW is in a series of actionable steps, as Jennifer Serravallo describes in *The Reading Strategies Book* (2015). One of our favorite ways to think about this is to break down the HOW into a series of three steps. This way, the strategy is procedural in nature—the students can follow the steps with or without you being there to guide them. It might sound like this:

> **THE WHAT + THE HOW** = Writers create paragraphs as they write stories by creating a new paragraph each time a character speaks.
>
> **1.** First, find a place in the writing where more than one character is speaking.
>
> **2.** Next, read the section aloud, making a mark every time you hear a new voice speaking.
>
> **3.** Then, rewrite the section, creating a new paragraph for each mark.

SOME EXAMPLES OF WHATS, OR SKILLS IN READING	SOME EXAMPLES OF WHATS, OR SKILLS IN WRITING
✿ Predict ✿ Summarize ✿ Determine Importance ✿ Visualize ✿ Infer ✿ Interpret ✿ Synthesize ✿ Analyze ✿ Critique	**Writing Process** ✿ Generate or collect entries (brainstorming). ✿ Rehearse or make a plan for a piece of writing. ✿ Write a rough draft. ✿ Revise a piece of writing. ✿ Edit a piece of writing. **Qualities of Strong Writing Structure** ✿ Make an outline for an essay or a story mountain for a narrative. ✿ Create paragraphs. ✿ Construct clear topic sentences. **Elaboration** ✿ Say more about a piece of evidence, an idea, a concept, a topic. ✿ Write descriptively. ✿ Use a balance of dialogue, actions, and inner thinking. **Conventions and Grammar** ✿ Use commas in a series. ✿ Create complex sentences. ✿ Maintain subject/verb agreement.

Other times, the HOW is just a quick way for students to figure out how to perform the desired skill. It might just sound like this:

> Writers create paragraphs as they write stories by creating a new paragraph when there is a change in setting—the subway arrives, the sun sets, a week goes by.

✤ Now, here is the bonus part. We have been at this place before, where it seems so simple and we launch into strategy writing. Sometimes, like in the example above, we are very familiar with the strategy, and with a bit of thinking we can name exactly HOW kids can practice a skill. But other times, after we have named the WHAT, we are less clear. "Okay," we think, "the what and the how. I know the what: I want my kids to find and interpret symbols when they read. Okay . . . now the how . . . the how . . . umm...."

How do we figure out the HOW if we don't know it automatically? How do we figure out the strategy, the way for kids to perform a skill? Here's the way that we learned to find the HOW.

Let's focus on a different example. The WHAT in this instance is the skill of interpreting a symbol in literature.

1. **Try to perform the skill yourself, as an adult, for a few minutes.** In this example, read a text or a part of the text and consider the symbols you see, thinking about their meaning. Give yourself five to ten minutes to try to perform the skill. Try it a few times or in a few places of a text.

   > *Example of performing the skill:* "I read a text and think, 'Huh, it seems like the fox is a symbol for anger and upset. Whenever he shows up in the book, it is always dark and stormy and the color red shows up over and over.'"

2. **Step back. Study what you did. Name how you did what you did.** Try to name exactly what you did as a reader or writer. Don't be afraid to be wordy at first! Try saying it a few different ways.

   > *Example of studying what you did:* "Well," I think. "I noticed that the fox was a symbol. I noticed that the fox popped up whenever there was trouble in the text. I also studied the images around the fox—the colors, the setting—to make me think what he might stand for."

   > *Example of naming how you did what you did:* "So, generally speaking, readers can interpret a symbol in a text by . . . looking for an image or color that shows up over and over again. Then they can ask themselves what the image or color might represent."

3. **Phrase the strategy in kid-friendly language. Be clear. Be explicit.** Make sure kids can understand each word and phrase. Remember, the goal is for them to do this work independently! Reach for kid-friendly language that describes exactly what you did.

   > *Example of phrasing the strategy in kid-friendly language:* "So to my class I could say that readers interpret symbols by finding repeating images or colors and asking themselves, 'What might these symbols really stand for? Could red really mean anger? Could the flying bird really stand for freedom?'"

This do-it-yourself process uncovers how one actually performs a reading or writing skill and helps name the strategy in a way that is teachable to others. It helps you figure out a HOW on your own. Plus, it is rooted in real writing and reading work so the HOWs you discover will feel authentic to you. Now, some strategies will be better than others, but doing the work yourself uncovers many possible strategies to try and use on your teaching tools and with your students.

Finally, think about WHY when putting the finishing touch on the strategy. Why is this strategy important? What is the purpose? Why might we, as readers or writers, want to do this work? We want to tether our skills and strategies to a strong sense of purpose. This helps students (and ourselves) buy into the work, know when to do the work, and see the bigger meaning of the work. The WHY is often verbal—a line or two of purpose spoken as the tool is unveiled. The WHY might sound something like this:

> **THE WHAT + THE HOW + THE WHY** = Writers create paragraphs in stories by making a new paragraph when there is a change in setting—the subway arrives, the sun sets, a week goes by. Paragraphs help readers get a visual heads-up about changes or shifts coming in the text, and they help them be ready to experience something new.

This process unlocks a floodgate of strategies. You can do this on your own or working with the company of colleagues. You can also do this work with kids, helping them to name the strategies they know and use.

Guided Practice: Crafting a Reading Strategy

Okay, first let's pick a WHAT. Let's imagine we want to get better at *inferring about characters*. And now we have to figure out the HOW, the strategies, or ways, to teach kids to do that big skill. **First, we need to practice that skill ourselves.** Right now, read the beginning of *Wonder* by R. J. Palacio. As you read, jot down initial ideas you have about this character:

> I know I'm not an ordinary ten-year-old kid. I mean, sure, I do ordinary things. I eat ice cream. I ride my bike. I play ball. I have an Xbox. Stuff like that makes me ordinary. I guess. And I feel ordinary. Inside. But I know ordinary kids don't make other ordinary kids run away screaming in playgrounds. I know ordinary kids don't get stared at wherever they go.
>
> If I found a magic lamp and I could have one wish, I would wish that I had a normal face that no one ever noticed at all. I would wish that I could walk down the street without people seeing me and then doing that look-away thing. Here's what I think: the only reason I'm not ordinary is that no one else sees me that way.
>
> But I'm kind of used to how I look by now. I know how to pretend I don't see the faces people make. We've all gotten pretty good at that sort of thing: me, Mom, and Dad, Via. Actually, I take that back: Via's

not so good at it. She can get really annoyed when people do something rude. . . .

. . . Via doesn't see me as ordinary. She says she does, but if I were ordinary, she wouldn't feel like she needs to protect me as much. And Mom and Dad don't see me as ordinary, either. They see me as extraordinary. I think the only person in the world who realizes how ordinary I am is me.

My name is August, by the way. I won't describe what I look like. Whatever you're thinking, it's probably worse.

> ### Evaluating the Importance of the Skill
>
> While you are practicing the skill, try naming why this work is important. Not only will this help you figure out the WHY to your strategy, it is also a good litmus test. If you can't name why this is important, it may not be the best skill to focus on!

What did you notice about August? What is he like? How would you describe him? What initial theories do you have about him?

Here's a quick example of what our notes looked like at this point:

> August seems like an ordinary kid. But it also seems like he knows he doesn't seem ordinary to other people. August seems like the kind of kid who is an outsider.

Now, second of all, step back. Study what you did. Name how you did what you did. We'll start off and study what we did. We tried to make inferences about the character in our notes above. So how did we do that? How did we arrive at that thinking?

Our notes:

> We noticed what the character liked and did for fun. But we also noticed how others reacted to the character. That's how we got to those thoughts about him seeming like an ordinary kid in some ways, but being an outsider in other ways.

Of course, your observations and theories will be different from ours, so you'll likely have arrived at them in different ways. Consider this: How did you arrive at your thinking in the previous step?

Okay, **lastly, try to phrase the strategy in kid-friendly language. Be clear. Be explicit.** We managed to uncover two strategies. Our notes:

> *Readers infer about a character by studying what he or she likes or does. These likes and dislikes, actions and activities reveal that character's personality and traits.*
>
> *Readers also infer about a character by studying how other characters react to him or her. These reactions reveal how the character deals with other people's reactions. This shows a big part of who he or she is as a person.*

You may find that your notes lead you to a completely different strategy, and that's great! Readers and writers need a range of strategies to choose from.

Put it all together (WHAT + HOW + WHY) and BOOM! You've developed your own teaching strategy, ready for sharing with students. Here's how we turned our thinking into a strategy:

> Readers make an inference about a character by studying what he or she likes or does. These likes and dislikes, actions and activities reveal the character's personality and traits. This is important because small things such as likes or actions often reveal big truths about people.

Once we have named our strategy, we can boil it down even further, getting it ready for, say, a repertoire chart or demonstration notebook. It can help to clarify what we are saying by breaking things down to a list of steps, like this:

> Readers make inferences about characters by . . .
>
> **1.** Studying their likes and dislikes
>
> **2.** Studying their actions and activities
>
> **3.** Asking, "What does this reveal about their personality?"

Fine-Tuning Your Strategies

In our years doing this work, we have stumbled across some obstacles along the way. Here are a few problems to be on the lookout for, and some ways to solve them when they arise:

☼ *First, be on the lookout for strategies that are too wordy.* This happens easily as we search for the exact words to name all that we are doing as a reader or writer. Too many words pose problems for the kids—they'll lose stamina as they read, the strategy won't fit on the teaching tool, they'll be less likely to remember it. If you find the strategy too wordy, try thinking of a catchphrase. It works in advertising. We are much more likely to remember Nike's slogan, "Just Do It," than "Just put aside all of your doubts and insecurities and seize the opportunity to do it!" Same rule applies with strategies: "make a movie in your mind" when you read, or "show, don't tell" when you write.

☼ *On a similar note, be on the lookout for strategies that are too general.* This problem is understandable. We, adult readers and writers, have a deep reservoir of knowledge of context and what things mean. So we'll write something like, "elaborate on the evidence," and although we know what that means and have ways to do that work, chances are many students will not. Instead, aim to be a bit more specific. How does one elaborate? What does elaboration mean? This way, "elaborate on the evidence" turns into "say more about the evidence—say it in a new way, give an example, or describe what it means." This increases the chances that students are able to do the strategy and to use the tool independently.

☼ *Finally, be on the lookout for cramming too much into one strategy or tool.* Reread the strategy and count how much is being asked of the student. A good rule of thumb is aiming for one skill and one strategy. Sometimes you'll find that you've discovered multiple strategies. This is a good thing! Just separate them into multiple strategies and teach them one at a time.

In Closing

In *The Wizard of Oz*, Dorothy meets friends who help her to find her way back home. Each one arrives at the right moment, offering advice and friendship and loyalty. And, just like Dorothy, throughout your journey with this work you'll find helpful friends along the way, friends who offer guidance, wisdom, and help. Keep these professional texts close at hand. Keep them at the ready to consult, become inspired by, use when you are stuck.

Glinda told Dorothy, at the end of her journey trying to get home by following the Yellow Brick Road, "You've always had the power, my dear. You had to learn it for yourself." In your journey with this work, channel the Good Witch of the North's advice. You have the power to find and name strategies because you are a reader and a writer. It's within you. You've had it all along.

Chapter Three

Remember This

Helping Students Recall Teaching

Right now I'm having amnesia and déjà vu at the same time.
I think I've forgotten this before.
—Steven Wright

How Can I Help Students Remember and Use What I Have Already Taught?

We've all been there.

> You sit back on your couch, dejected. A pile of notebooks crowds around you, entries and stacks of sticky notes on each open page. You shake your head as you read notebook after notebook full of work that you feel your class should have moved beyond by now, character analysis limited to insights like, "She is sad," or simple retellings of chapters. While you would be okay with this work in, say, third grade, these were your sixth-graders! In February! After months of teaching! "I've taught them so much more than this!" you think to yourself, and then go into the kitchen to grab another cookie.

As teachers, we've all had that moment when, looking at student work, we struggled to find evidence of our teaching. Instead of seeing the newer, shinier work of the unit reflected in students' writing or reading, we see the comfortable, worn-in moves students have been doing for years. Often when students write or read, they default to what feels most comfortable. They rely on a strategy they found success with at one point in their schooling, or they grab onto whatever first comes to mind, especially when working independently. In fact, we would argue that it is quite rare indeed to find a child who, independent of any tool or support, stops in his or her tracks before putting pen to paper and thinks, "Wait a second, I bet there is a strategy Ms. Roberts taught me in the last few months that would help me do my best work," and then rifles through oodles of notes to look for the strategy that can help him or her work hardest.

And who can blame them? A student's day is filled with layer upon layer of information. Just think about what the kids in your class have to sift through on any given day in school:

- ☼ Four to six lessons across different subject areas (and, if departmentalized, different teachers)

- ☼ Instructions for how to do everything from walk the halls to perform an experiment, which may vary from teacher to teacher

- ☼ The texts, stories, and examples shared in each of their classes

- ☼ The texts, stories, projects, and examples they are generating or working on in each class

- ☼ Individualized feedback from all of their other teachers

- ☼ An array of pleasant, exciting, and/or terrifying and mildly traumatizing social interactions.

In graduate school, Kate was once asked to follow a student throughout the day. During each class she scrambled to take notes: dates, equations, scientific explanations, and writing strategies filled pages with each new hour of instruction. Soon she noticed a refrain from the teachers, phrases like, "I've taught this before," "You've learned this already," and "You should know this by now." By eighth period, she was struck by two things—the tidal wave of ideas and facts coming at kids all day long, and the undercurrent of slight annoyance as kids struggled to immediately remember prior teaching.

There was a palpable tension between the sheer volume of information the student encountered in a day and the assumption of quick recall and application. Kate felt a nervous ping in her stomach. If *she* felt daunted to remember all this information in a day, how could this wonderful, somewhat scattered middle-school student remember all of it?

It's possible that the ability to automatically recall wide swaths of data is less useful to us now. While few dispute the importance of knowing some things, of having information at our fingertips, there is growing debate about how important it is to spend time being sure that kids have memorized, say, the state capitals, when we are living in the age of smartphones. This is not so much of a *new* conversation; Albert Einstein, too, wondered at the usefulness of memorization when he said, "Never memorize something that you can look up in a book." Now, with what Einstein would have considered supercomputers at our fingertips, this quote has an even louder ring. In *How We Learn*, Benedict Carey

(2015) takes this idea a step further. Citing decades of research on learning, he asserts that, in fact, forgetting information is a vital part of the learning process, an integral way that our brains decide over time which new information to hold onto. These theorists urge us to accept and even, at times, celebrate our students' lack of memorization.

At the same time, kids do need to remember information over the course of their studies and their lives. When we teach students to read nonfiction and they do not remember or use any strategies for figuring out tough vocabulary, it is a problem, mainly one of efficiency and automaticity. When students craft a piece of writing and don't hold onto any prior lessons on structure or conventions, it is a problem. Just as a soccer player needs to have the moves of a corner kick in her bones, over time a reader must own the moves of reading and writing. But this process—of learning things so that they become automatic—is a more complex one than simply memorizing some information. Instead, we find that students need support, time, and repetition to make learning stick.

Your students *can* be more thoughtful about what strategies they use in their reading and writing, and they *can* hold onto your teaching as time goes on. They just need a little help.

Charts Help Students Remember What You Have Taught Them

If you find yourself in this situation—students don't seem to be recalling earlier learning—a chart of past teaching might be the right teaching tool for the job. Here, we offer a lesson we have taught across classrooms when using charts to help students remember what they have been taught. Specifically, this lesson centers around a class that needs help holding onto all of the ways it has been taught to think about and analyze a character in a book.

We begin the lesson by naming the bigger issue and connecting it to something personal, in this case, our experience on the couch. "Class, I have to have a talk with you today. I read through your notebooks last night, and while I saw how hard you have been working, and how much you have kept up with writing about your reading, what I did not see were . . . my lessons." (A slight dramatic pause, a wrinkled nose, or a sad look in the eyes works well here to communicate the feeling of slight disappointment or playful disbelief.) "I care that you try out some of the things I teach you, not just because I have spent time on my lessons, but because I really

---

Assessing the Situation: How Do I Know Whether Helping Students Recall Teaching Is the Issue?

Your students may need teaching tools to help them remember your teaching if:

1. When it comes time for independent work, students look lost, or ask you, "What do you want me to do?"

2. Student work looks like the same move over and over again. For instance, a student's writing is heavy in dialogue even though you have taught an entire collection of narrative craft writing moves. Or, in reading, a student's collection of jots is all centered around one thing, such as a character's emotions.

3. During one-on-one conferences, you notice that your students wait for you to tell them what to do and don't offer up much themselves. Your conferences feel a bit like pulling teeth, or holding an interrogation. ("What are you writing about? Your birthday party? Who was there? Your mother? What's she like?") Sometimes this is because students can't recall the language or lessons of your curriculum.

believe that if you do this work you will love reading even more than you do now. That you'll get what I call 'reader chills'—that feeling when you have had a huge, awesome thought about a book. It's the kind of thought that feels like discovering something new, like a secret level in a video game or a secret sale at your favorite shoe store."

Then, we are sure to name the purpose of today's work, along with a good dose of confidence that we can do better. "I realized that I have spent so much time trying to teach what I think are the *best* strategies for you to use for your reading, but what I haven't done yet is to help you *remember* to use them. No wonder my lessons didn't show up in your notebooks! Well, we are going to fix that today. We are going to make a chart together of the greatest hits of our year so far—the strategies that we think are just the most helpful ones. I'm going to start us off, but make sure each of you thinks of another strategy that you believe would really help you think more deeply about your books."

We reveal a piece of chart paper with the heading "Let's Read Using All We Know!" and say, "So I am thinking about my own reading life, and how, when I'm reading on auto-pilot, I default to thinking about my characters' feelings and some simple traits about them. But the thing is, I know I can do more than that. One thing we learned in this unit is that when we want to deepen our thinking about the characters in our books, we can think about how they interact with other characters, and what their relationships are like. So I'm going to write that down on our chart." In front of the class we write one of the strategies we planned earlier to include. Figure 3–1 shows sixth-grade teacher Leigh Anne Eck's example of the beginning of a repertoire chart when teaching a lesson similar to this one.

"And we also learned that we can think about how a character is changing and what causes him or her to change. Do you remember that?" We add that strategy to the list, and then turn it over to the class. "Okay, so now it's up to you. Think about what you have learned in this unit. Turn and talk to the person next to you—what is your favorite lesson so far?"

As the class begins to talk, we circle the room, listening into conversations,

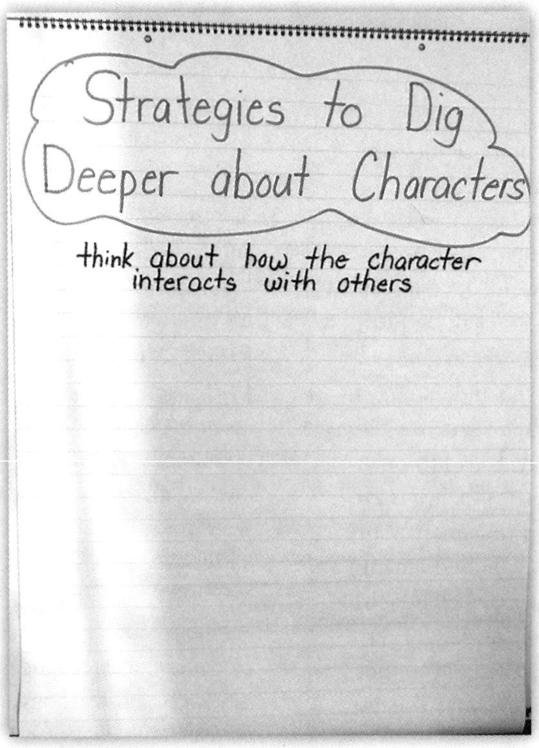

Figure 3–1 An example of a repertoire chart in process from Leigh Anne Eck's sixth-grade class at George Rogers Clark Middle School in Vincennes, Indiana. Using shorthand captures the essence of the reading or writing strategies, providing a brief reminder, or tag line, to spark kids' memories.

holding close in our mind the list of strategies we expect kids might remember. We are sure to listen for hints of these "greatest hits" strategies, sometimes even coaxing kids a bit to name them themselves. Soon we gather everyone's attention and highlight some of the strategies that students named. "Great! Here are a couple of things I heard. This partnership said that they liked the strategy where we thought about the emotions that characters have and how they change across the book. And, over here, these two said that they remembered how we looked at what motivates characters to act the way they do, or be the way they are. I'm going to add those to our chart now." Figure 3–2 shows Leigh Anne's chart as she collected ideas and gave credit to the kids who named them.

After finishing writing, we continue. "Okay, so today you are going to keep reading, but I want you to think a little bit about which of the things we wrote down on the chart will most help you have the most interesting thoughts about your book. Talk it out with your partner."

As the class begins to talk, we listen in and coach students. We ask some students to discuss why they chose one strategy over another, pushing them to name what exactly in their book guided them to that strategy. We coach others to choose something, anything, as a way to get started, gently reassuring them that whatever strategy they choose will most likely work.

Bringing the class together one last time, we are sure to compliment them. We believe in creating "high-five" energy whenever possible, the feeling that we are proud of what our kids have offered. We then say, "When I teach you something to think about in your reading, I am not just asking you to do that work today and then never do it again. I really

> **Reminder: How to Make a Repertoire Chart**
>
> (For a more detailed look at how to make a chart, refer to Chapter Two.)
>
> **STEP ONE:** Make a heading around a skill or goal.
>
> **STEP TWO:** List the strategies, or ways, your students can work toward that skill or goal, preferably with other students.
>
> **STEP THREE:** Hang the chart in an accessible place and refer to it often.

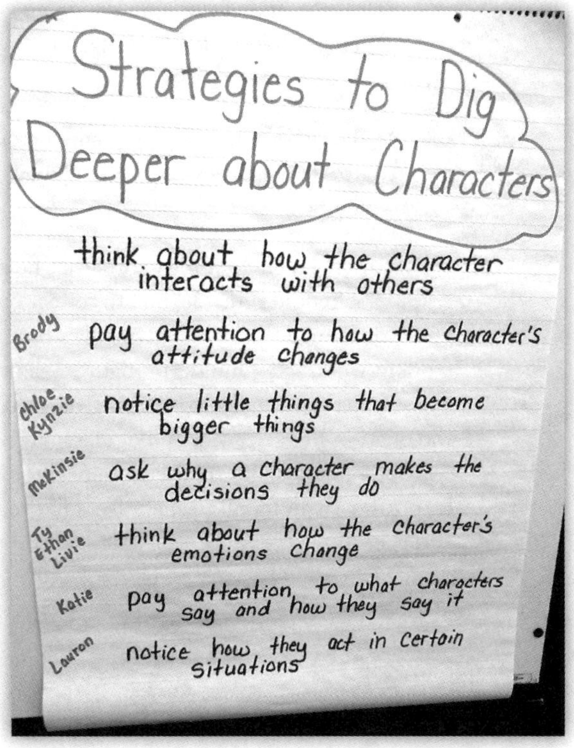

Figure 3–2 An example of a repertoire chart co-constructed with students. Attaching students' names to strategies highlights the strengths of each student, as well as empowers students to be intellectual leaders who can help others with work they feel strong in.

Strategies to Dig Deeper about Characters

think about how the character interacts with others

Brody pay attention to how the character's attitude changes

Chloe Kynzie notice little things that become bigger things

McKinsie ask why a character makes the decisions they do

Ty Ethan Livie think about how the character's emotions change

Katie pay attention to what characters say and how they say it

Lauren notice how they act in certain situations

do hope that you will fold some of my lessons into your reading forever, that some of these strategies will become a part of you. So today, as you read and write about your reading, I want you to keep your strategy in mind. Of course, you can also choose other things to think about, but it will help you to have a focus to begin with today."

After a lesson like this, we have confidence that the day will go more smoothly, that students will try their chosen strategies, and that, for the day, their notebooks and sticky notes will reflect the teaching. But we also know that unless we keep this chart in clear focus, the class will probably stray from using it, and their work might revert back. In the spirit of keeping the work vibrant and helping students remember new work to try, here are a few ways to keep a chart alive for students during a unit:

- ☼ Every day, while the students read independently, interrupt them and remind them to check in on the chart and think about how it could help their writing-about-reading work.

- ☼ For every lesson taught, add that strategy to a class chart, helping students see that the lessons taught become work they are expected to choose from when they read.

- ☼ During the end of class, ask students to talk with a partner about which strategies they used during class that day and which ones they will use that night.

- ☼ At the end of the unit, create an assessment that reflects the strategies on the chart. Tell students this is one way that they will be assessed on what they learned during the unit.

- ☼ During conferences and small groups, refer to the chart often, asking students to say what they are working on as readers and using the chart as a starting point.

Your efforts in creating charts that help kids recall teaching will yield some uplifting results. Schedule yourself time to reflect on student work in the days and weeks to come after you launch this work in your classrooms. Keep your eyes peeled to find and celebrate student work, like Jenna's (in Figure 3–3 on page 44), a sixth-grader in Leigh Anne Eck's class, who began analyzing the motivations of the characters in her books after co-creating the chart in Figure 3–2 with her class. Harvest the fruits of your teaching, share the work with other colleagues, and celebrate the big and small leaps publically in the classroom by posting them for all to see. After all, everyone, no matter the age, loves to see the footprints of his or her progress.

How to Set Goals and Narrow Our Focus

For this lesson, we identified the teaching our students were not holding onto or employing when working independently. This became our ultimate goal for the chart: to help our students remember how to analyze the characters in their books. To set this goal, we did the following things:

1. First, we looked at student work that was done *independently*. We chose student work to study that was done without too much teacher-directed coaching and in response to texts students could read independently. (This was a reading lesson. If it were writing, we could have chosen notebook entries or a draft.) Studying their reading notebook entries was a good place to see what work the class held onto (or not) from day to day, week to week.

2. Next, we compared the student work to prior teaching. We scanned the body of student work and investigated what lessons the students held onto and internalized and what lessons did not show up. This meant we had to forego the myriad of other lenses we could use to assess student work. Our primary, guiding question was, "What evidence of my teaching do I see in this student work?" And when we did not see the traction of our lessons, we set goals for the chart.

3. Last, we decided which lessons to hold students to. Once we determined the places our teaching wasn't sticking, we had to make some tough decisions. Which lessons felt the most important? It seems unrealistic to say to kids, "You will remember every single thing I say." Instead, we prioritized. We did this by looking for the lessons or strategies that felt like "power moves." Which lessons would really transform our students' work? We were sure to include a range of lessons in terms of sophistication. This way, our chart would include strategies that both our more emergent students could use, as well as our advanced readers.

Knowing this chart would be made in front of the class, we understood the importance of determining what teaching to highlight for students ahead of time. By having this predetermined list in our mind, we could be sure to identify the most important teaching, while creating an organic feel for constructing the chart together.

How to Assess Whether Students Remembered
(*and Whether the Teaching Tools Worked*)

One way to assess how well your teaching tools are working to help students remember your teaching is to check in along the way with a formative assessment (meaning an assessment that gives you information to help form your teaching, not as a grade or final evaluation). On-demand performance assessments can be incredibly helpful in seeing which of your students are using the teaching tools being offered to them.

Here is an example of one formative assessment you can give to students to see how well they are holding onto your teaching.

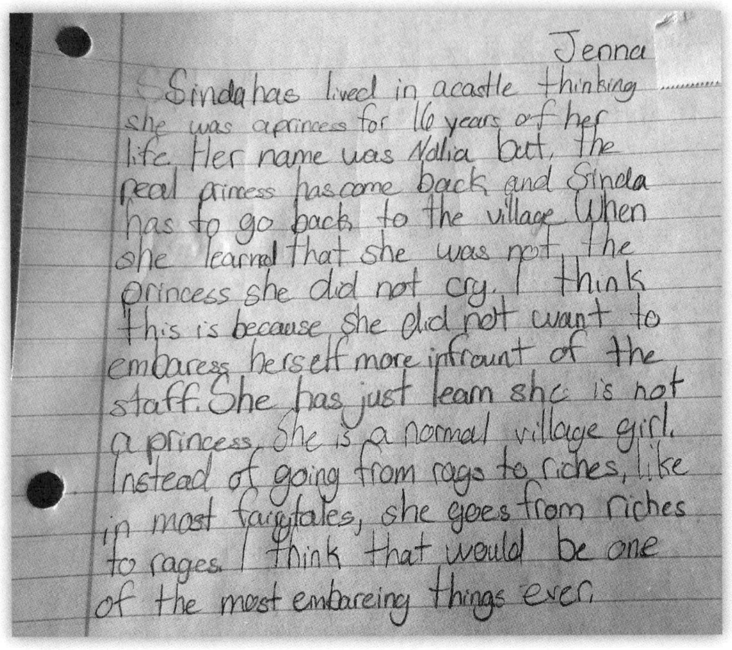
Jenna
Sinda has lived in acastle thinking
she was aprincess for 16 years of her
life. Her name was Nalia but, the
real princess has come back and Sinda
has to go back to the village. When
she learned that she was not the
princess she did not cry. I think
this is because she did not want to
embaress herself more infrount of the
staff. She has just learn she is not
a princess. She is a normal village girl.
Instead of going from rags to riches, like
in most fairytales, she goes from riches
to rages. I think that would be one
of the most embareing things ever.

Figure 3–3 Jenna's Writing About Reading After Using a Chart to Remember Strategies

For Reading:

1. Collect a few short texts, or passages from texts, that span, generally, the reading levels in your room. (If you "quiz" your class on texts that are too hard, you are simply testing their reading levels instead of their reading skill proficiency.)
2. Create some generalized questions or prompts that mirror the current unit and could relate to any story (such as "Describe what kind of person the character is . . ." or "Discuss one possible theme emerging in this text . . .").
3. Decide whether or not to cover up or take away the teaching tools students have been using. If you take them away, we suggest giving your students some warning so they can "study up." If you leave them, you are assessing, in part, whether they use them when needed or not.
4. Give the assessment to your class after they have read the appropriate passage.
5. Look for growth in their work.

For Writing:

Same as for reading, but instead of texts and prompts, you will just need a prompt that fits the work you are asking students to remember, such as "Write the introduction and first paragraph of an essay about something or someone you love and why you love them" or "Pick a topic you know well and draft the table of contents for a report you could write about that topic."

Other Tools to Help Students Remember What You Have Taught

Charts are incredibly helpful for recording your teaching. In making a chart, you create an artifact that serves as a reminder and guide for students when they have lost their way. But charts are not the only tools that help refresh a student's memory. In fact, depending on how you use them, many if not all of the tools described in Chapter Two can be used to keep your teaching in the forefront of your students' minds.

USE BOOKMARKS TO CREATE A PERSONALIZED LIST OF WHAT TO REMEMBER

While the teacher's chart can be an invaluable tool to help students hold onto teaching, another great way to remember something is to make the list yourself. Someone else's ideas of what is important will never stick to you as much as your own. Similarly, when a teacher is making a chart, he is necessarily thinking about all of the students in his class. That means there are, most likely, many items or steps on the chart that will not be helpful to a particular learner simply due to his or her particular needs and abilities. Having students make bookmarks—personalized lists of things that will help them to remember past teaching—will allow your class to decide which lessons, which tips and strategies and ideas, they most want to remember.

Take this example: It is that time of the year again. The state literacy test is on the horizon. You are spending time supporting your kids as test takers and coming up with ways to increase confidence when tackling challenges, like the state test. The trouble is, every year you notice that, come test time, your students don't actually use many of the strategies you taught. They *don't* reread the passage or go back to check their answers. They *don't* pace themselves or work strategically. They seem to charge through the test like stressed-out bulls, hoping to get to the end. Your students are not holding onto the lessons they have learned.

While a chart might help, bookmarks make the work more personal. Here is how to help students make bookmarks of their favorite strategies.

1. First, make sure that kids have access to all of the lessons taught. Make sure that charts are up, that kids have their notebooks open with a partner, and that any handouts are in easy reach.

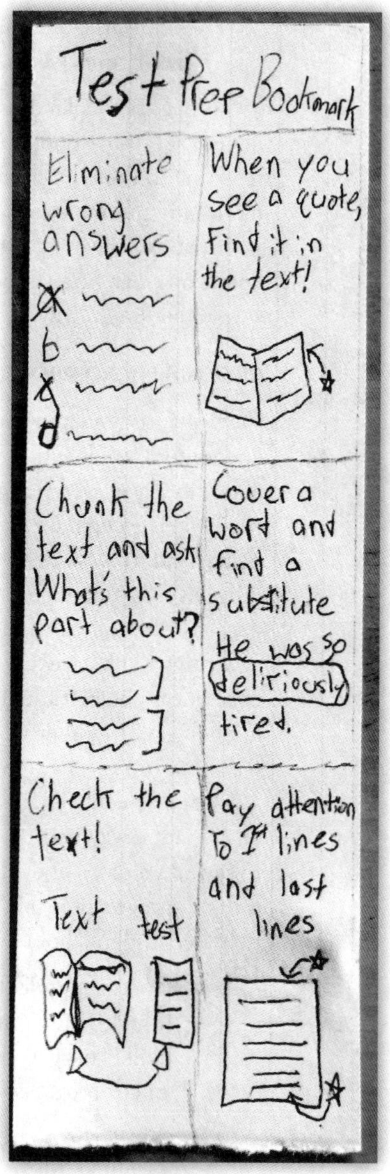

Figure 3–4 Cole's Bookmark for Test-Taking Strategies

2. Then, show the class how to look across all of this teaching and select the things that most help you. Begin a bookmark in front of the class.

3. Lastly, give students time and coaching (plus paper and pens and colored pencils) to make their own bookmarks, with support. Students have the charts and notes and handouts, a partner to talk to, and you to help them if they get that "deer in the headlights" look. Like Cole, a seventh-grader in Medfield, Massachusetts, did, encourage your students to represent their strategies with icons or figures (see Figure 3–4).

Once the bookmarks are made, the work can begin. Throughout the unit, have students keep those bookmarks next to them—during lessons, practice work, and so on—referring to them consistently. The week before the test, students can retire their bookmarks and put them away, but not before naming which strategies worked best for them.

Just as a chart can help strengthen your students' grasp on what has been taught, bookmarks can be a support for students who may need a more personalized list, one that stays quite literally by their side for as long as they need the support.

CREATE A MICRO-PROGRESSION TO PRIORITIZE CERTAIN SKILLS FOR STUDENTS

We want students to remember what we have taught them. This is a given. However, we encounter trouble when we teach too much to hold onto, too much to remember. Think about it: if you were taught a new lesson a day, without pause, at some point you would not be able to hold on anymore. The wheels of your learning would come off from such a heavy load. If we treat each new lesson or skill as *equally important* as all the others, it is difficult for students to prioritize what is being taught and what to remember.

Instead, we can help students hold onto our teaching by deciding which reading or writing skills in each unit are the most essential for students to learn. We can then continue to hold students accountable to these skills, as opposed to everything and the kitchen sink. In other words, keep it simple and get it right. Micro-progressions can help with that work.

Sarah Reedy, an instructional coach in Brooklyn, New York, decided in her seventh-grade essay unit that the most important skill for her kids to focus on was the ability to say *how* a piece of evidence supports an idea. Valuing this skill, Sarah decided to create a micro-progression that she repeatedly used across the unit, knowing that this would help her students hold onto and *remember* this skill. Here is how she did it:

1. First, she reflected on her kids, using student work, and determined what a high-, medium-, and low-level version of this work looked like around the skill. This gave her some parameters and gave her a sense of the range for her micro-progression.

2. Then, she named what the work was at each level—what the criteria were for reaching this particular skill level—and articulated this work in kid-friendly language. She consulted resources such as professional texts, colleagues, and her own writing when she got stuck for content.

3. Finally, for each level of skill she drafted a model from a familiar text or topic that showed the work at that level. She made sure to highlight the part of the work that she wanted her students to notice.

Sarah decided to make the micro-progression in front of her kids, knowing this would be more powerful, so she made sure she was super familiar with the micro-progression before beginning the lesson (see Figure 3–5). The next day

The death penalty is wrong because people are killed. In fact, 188 death row inmates have been found innocent. This shows the death penalty is wrong because innocent people are killed.	The death penalty is wrong because innocent people are killed. In fact, 188 death row inmates have been found innocent. This shows that in fact there are people who have been wrongfully accused and killed for a crime they did not commit. This means that the death penalty is wrong because innocent people should not be killed by the government.	The death penalty is wrong because innocent are killed. In fact, 188 death row inmates have been found innocent. These are innocent people who are going to be put to death. The possibility of state-sponsored murder is unacceptable. Because of this – and because there is no way to promise no innocent lives will be lost – the death penalty must not continue.
• Repeats the topic sentence or claim as your analysis • Uses the same language as your topic sentence or claim.	• Attempts to explain how the evidence supports the idea. • May use prompts or transitional language	• Highlights or unpacks the parts of the evidence—that BEST supports the idea. • Plays with language, syntax and word choice for greatest effect.

Figure 3–5 Sarah Reedy's Micro-progression on Analyzing Evidence

she revealed the micro-progression with only the bottom—the lean list of qualities—filled out. Then, with her class, she guided them through her thinking about the models on top, allowing for their feedback. This shared writing experience helped her class feel that they understood and owned the micro-progression, instead of it simply being presented to them by their teacher.

LEAN ON A DEMONSTRATION NOTEBOOK TO REINFORCE TEACHING

Sometimes it's not that we don't remember the name of something, it's just that the details are fuzzy. A chart can help us say, "Oh, right! I could always stretch out the important part of my writing," but it may not help us remember *how* to do that thing. Just think about it: as a kid, you might remember that riding a bike is something you could do, but you might have forgotten how it works to actually get on it and ride. This is why it helps to have repeated demonstrations when we learn things like riding a bike or reading poetry—to help us remember the *how* of a thing, not just the *what*. Demonstration notebooks can support students who need an additional round of seeing how a lesson or strategy works before it becomes their own, before it becomes internalized.

While studying student writing with a group of fifth-grade teachers on Staten Island, New York, Maggie and the team noticed a handful of young writers still struggling in the midst of a narrative writing unit. The teachers had taught their students how to zoom in on the most important moments in their stories, but this group of writers was still telling stories that covered such a huge swath of time that it was hard to see the meaning within all the plot. Maggie and the teachers wondered if the students needed help remembering how exactly, as a writer, to zoom in on the most important parts of a story.

After the study group, the teachers pulled the students they flagged as needing more support and gathered them around Maggie's demonstration notebook. Maggie began by saying, "So I know you know that when we write stories, we zoom in on the most important part we want to write about. I think practicing a bit more might help us to remember how to do that in our writing. What do you think?"

Maggie went to her demonstration page (Figure 3–6), showing them how she could take her story about the week she went to Cape Cod and narrow it down to just ten minutes of that vacation.

First, Maggie read them her original story, at the top of the page. When she was done she pointed out how her story covered the entire vacation. "That kind of 'all about my trip' writing is okay for a summary, but when we tell stories we want to stretch out smaller important moments to make sure we show *all* of the meaning and details we experienced. We want to take our readers on a journey with our stories, not just tell them quickly all about what we did." She continued, "There are three main ways I can focus on the most important part of my story. Check it out. First, I can narrow it down to an important ten-minute moment. Second, I can spotlight a moment when I felt something really strongly. Or, lastly, I can focus on a part where something changed. Let's practice on my piece together." Maggie quickly demonstrated using one strategy to narrow the focus of her story, retelling just a ten-minute moment. Afterward, Maggie and the group voted on another strategy to try and practiced how that could sound in writing all together. Then, Maggie handed each student a sticky note and said, "Now try the same thing in your notebooks. What is the most important part of your story?" As the kids began picking a strategy and rewriting the moment, Maggie went around and quickly coached each student to support their transition into his or her own writing.

Following a lesson using a demonstration notebook, kids can take an additional sticky note and write a reminder of the strategy they'd like to try and prac-

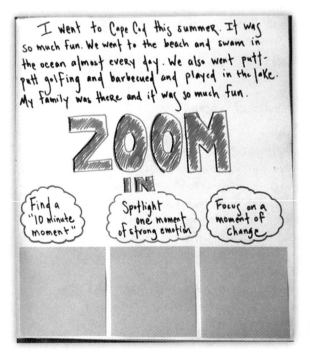

Figure 3-6 Sample Demonstration Notebook Page

tice more independently. This way, writers leave with tangible reminders of the lesson, as well as a written intention of future practice. This quick goal setting helps students be more attached to their homework as they are a participant in their next steps.

Knowing the Way:
When Will They Be Ready to Give Up the Teaching Tool?

Of course, our ultimate goal is not that kids need teaching tools to remember your teaching. Just as you eventually take that first car ride where you don't consult your road map or use the GPS, we want students to have the experience of automaticity with their learning. Our ultimate goal is for students to not need these tools—these scaffolds—anymore. This means that you and your students will have to find opportunities to take the tools away and see what happens. Here are some common opportunities:

1. **Timing:** Try taking away the teaching tools at certain points in the unit, perhaps after a few days, a few weeks, or even at the end of the unit. Or challenge students to set goal times themselves for when they'll graduate from the teaching tool. Coach students to veer away from the teaching tool after using it a number of times.

2. **Behavioral Cues:** Be on the lookout for certain behavioral cues to show when a teaching tool has been internalized. Notice whether or not students' eyes travel to the tool immediately when they begin working independently. Take an informal poll to gather stats on the charts that are used daily, often, at times, or not at all. Have students vote on which charts to "retire" and replace with new ones.

3. **Rigor:** Challenge students to a day without using their tools. One way to try this is challenging the entire class to do the day's work without a specific chart, perhaps the one you made at the beginning of the week. Another is for students to self-nominate a chart to give up for the day's work. Or, students can set challenges for each other to test whether the teaching stuck or not.

Not Quite Ready . . .?

These check-ins are designed to see how students do without the support of a teaching tool and to see whether or not they are ready to work without it. Inevitably, we have to be prepared if students are not quite ready to give up the tool.

Be on the lookout for signs that students are not ready to work without guidance. When you take away a teaching tool, pay close attention to how students react. Some will flourish, while others may flounder. Be ready to return the tool to students needing more time, setting a future date when you will again see how they perform without it.

Quick Tip for Going Digital

If you have a classroom blog, you can use it to post photos of your charts or other popular tools for students to use outside of class. This encourages students and parents to use these tools independently, as well as creating a record of your teaching. Class blogs used as keepers of reminder charts or micro-progressions then become a virtual notebook for your class—a resource for students wherever they are working.

This virtual notebook can be an incredible time saver. Instead of taking up loads of class time having students copy notes or charts in our room, they can use that time to do more appropriate and challenging work. Like Jess Lifshitz, who curates the useful charts in her room and posts them for students to use.

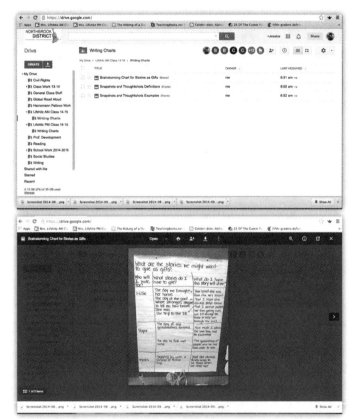

Figure 3–7 Many educators have used a virtual communal space (such as Google Drive) or blogging platforms (such as Blogger, Edublogs, or Kidblog) to set up their class blog.
Google and the Google logo are registered trademarks of Google, Inc., used with permission.

In addition to storing charts online for easy access, technology can also help us find ways to translate our charts into other mediums to make them even more accessible. Third-grade teacher Sarah Anthony at PS 59 took a photo of a chart that Maggie had made with her class, and then used a sticky-note printing template to turn that chart into sticky notes (see Figure 3–8). This way, Sarah could offer kids their own personal chart to reference right in their notebooks, books, or desk.

Quick Tip for Going Digital (continued)

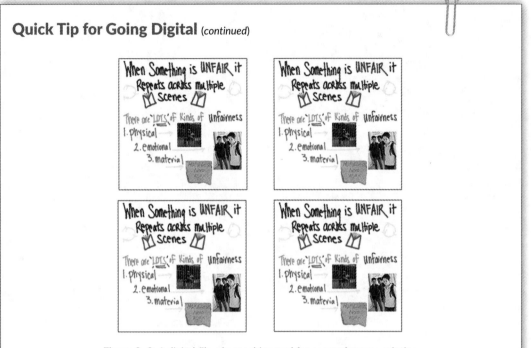

Figure 3–8 A digital file of a teaching tool for easy reference, printing, and sharing, inside or outside the classroom.

In Closing

It is tempting to fall into the trap of getting exasperated when students do not remember past teaching. Before we know it, we have rolled our eyes and said, "But I already taught you that!" However, as educators from Christopher Lehman to M. Colleen Cruz remind us, if we had really taught it, then the kids would be able to do it. They would have *learned*. When our students shrug at the mention of past lessons, instead of allowing this natural frustration to take hold, we can work to see that what our students are really doing is communicating with us. They are saying, "I'm not quite there yet, I'm having trouble holding on." And even more importantly, when we hear our students communicating this to us, we can *help*.

Chapter Four

You Can Do It

Motivating Students to Work Hard

Whenever I feel the need to exercise,
I lie down until it goes away.
—Paul Terry

How Can I Support Rigor in My Classroom?

We want our students to take their work to the "next level," but how do we get there?

You know that familiar noise—the sound of a class starting to lose focus. There's the murmur of side conversations, the unnecessary rustling of papers, the little snaps of pens inexplicably falling to the floor. In these moments, you look up, your suspicions confirmed. The kids are distracted. You address the situation right away: "What's up, writers?" There are shrugs, but you press on. "Something must be up if you have stopped working." Silence, and then a familiar, "We're done?" Nods of agreement follow. You feel a wave of frustration—the work ahead is complex and time consuming. How could they be done? You glance at their notebook pages and indeed they have "finished" the task at hand, but only the least sophisticated version of the work you set out for the class to tackle. You sigh and muster a defeated, "But we are NEVER done writing."

Rigor is a tricky word. Few fight the idea that we want students to be able to roll up their sleeves and work hard on something challenging. We view this as one of the fundamental tasks of school—helping students along the way as they develop a strong work ethic. In fact, the ability to be persistent and focused, reaching the highest level of performance personally possible, is a critical ingredient for success in any field. Then there is the recent, popular fear that the work in schools for the past few decades has *not* been rigorous enough. A recent study by the Center for Public Education found that if we measure rigor by how well our school system is preparing kids for college and beyond, then by some measurements our schools are not, in fact, rigorous enough. These factors have created an educational climate today whereby it is difficult to read much about education without seeing a mention of rigor thrown into the mix. In some ways, this spotlight on rigor could be a good thing. Increased discussion around how to help students learn to want to work harder is undoubtedly positive. Creating an educational climate that elevates the level of thinking, discussion, and performance is ideal when raising the next generation.

Conversations around rigor often take two forms. The first focuses on how difficult *the task* is that students are being asked to accomplish. There are many ways to make a task more rigorous: elevate the text complexity, raise the standards, increase the volume of writing. Studies around academic complexity have propelled a national conversation and debate on the value or harm in raising academic benchmarks, increasing text complexity, and creating higher-level comprehension standards (Council of Chief State School Officers and National Governors Association n.d.). Yet a conversation around rigor that centers on the difficulty level of the task or text leaves out the performance, engagement, and agency of the learner.

Alternatively, we focus on the second form of rigor as a description of a behavior rather than a description of a task. Rigor is performative—it is a stance, an action, a state of being that is taken to move through the world, tackle tasks, or work toward a goal. And when we focus on the work and effort that students put into tackling a task and not just the task itself, we create opportunities to really see what's difficult for kids. For instance, when studying students' performance, often we see that kids stop short, feeling as though their work is "good enough," when really they have just scratched the surface. In her galvanizing book *Mindset: The New Psychology of Success*, Carol S. Dweck (2006) emphasizes the importance of students seeing themselves as always working toward a new goal, of having a learner's mind, a growth mindset. As she says so poetically, "becoming is better than being."

We know when we see this rigor of becoming in our classrooms. Think for a moment of a time your students worked rigorously. Perhaps their attention was concentrated and unwavering as the bell rung. Maybe students kept at it as problems arose, imagining different solutions with a series of "Maybe let's try this!" or "Could it be this?" Or there was a lively focus in the room, a palpable buzz of curiosity. But we also know full well what it looks like when this rigor is absent. Again, think for a moment, this time on a time when rigor was missing. Perhaps students completed their work so quickly that you barely finished the lesson before you heard, "How long does this have to be?" or "Is this good enough?" or "I'm done." Or maybe you looked out onto the sea of slumped shoulders and heads resting on the desks. Or perhaps the lack of effort showed in the writing assignments littered with texting language or little punctuation.

A rigor problem like this is not going to be solved by simply raising the complexity of the task. As Kylene Beers (2014) has tweeted, "rigor without relevance is simply hard." Instead, we can focus on how to teach and support kids in their quest to nurture their inner confidence and become *harder workers*. That is, we can create a learning climate where students see the steps needed to tackle the tasks in front of them rigorously and believe that they can have success along the way—a learning climate that clearly shows what is gained by putting in the hard work to tackle something challenging and achieve something great. Daniel Pink explores ways to create this climate in his book *Drive* (2009). He posits that only by tapping into and nurturing intrinsic motivation within students will they achieve great things. One of the keys to increasing this motivation, he says, is to create a sense of autonomy, a sense of *I know what to do*. "Control leads to compliance; autonomy leads to engagement," Pink states, and reading this we might have to admit that much of our teaching still leans on telling students what to do rather than fostering the idea that they can succeed on their own. To truly support students in working harder, we will have to offer them a clear vision for what that rigorous work looks like, each step of the way.

It also means that we must have faith in our students. We will have to dismiss the predictable initial judgments that can drift into our thoughts when we are frustrated, like describing students that are not working hard as lazy, lethargic, or unmotivated. Instead, we can pause to reflect on the possibility that students simply might not know what exactly is being expected of them, or they may not understand the steps to take to do rigorous work or believe that they can get there. For example, while growing up, Kate was often asked to vacuum the floors to help her mother out around the house. She liked the challenge of this chore. But afterward her mother would be frustrated. "That was too fast," she said. But Kate didn't understand, because to her the floor looked clean. She didn't know what the floors would look like if they were rigorously vacuumed—behind the sofa, under the throw rugs, up the stairs. So she didn't know what else to do with the leftover time besides pretend to vacuum what seemed already clean. Similarly, students often don't know what to keep working on when they finish a task or are not able to visualize ways to improve it.

Students can learn how to work more rigorously, but they need guidance to help them along the way.

Assessing the Situation: Signals That Rigor May Be the Issue

Your students may need teaching tools to help them work harder. Consider the following situations.

1. Students can accomplish a reasonable level of work when asked explicitly to do so. However, without your prompting and pressure, the work in the room falls flat.

2. Students seem to finish their work at lightning speed and then wait for you to tell them whether it is good enough to be done. You notice a consistent lack of reflection or self-assessment.

3. You study student work across a span of days, weeks, or months and do not see an arc of growth, despite noticing that students can do better when pushed.

Micro-progressions Help Students See How to Work Harder

When we have faced a class that is not working as hard as we have hoped, we often turn to a micro-progression to give a vision of what that hard work looks like. Our lessons follow in the footsteps of the lesson below. In this specific example, we work on nonfiction writing with a class of freshmen.

We begin by naming the issue while keeping our tone light. Kids generally don't mind being told there is a problem, but when they feel like we disapprove of them or are frustrated, they can shut down. We want to keep the doors open. So we say, "Do you remember how yesterday we kind of hit a wall together? I wanted you to keep working, and to work harder, and you kind of gave me this expression like, 'Um, we don't know what you are talking about.'" We inevitably laugh a little bit, both to lighten the mood and also to gently, lovingly make fun of the situation. "Yeah. Well, at first I have to admit, I was frustrated. But then I realized, you might not know what it looks like to work really, really hard on your nonfiction pieces of writing! Like, I know I taught you that one of the most important things a nonfiction writer might do is to describe things in vivid detail, and that's great, but what does it look like to do a really, *really* good job on that? To put your all into it and really hit it out of the park, like a home run?"

"Today I want to create something with you that we can use all year long, in writing class but also in social studies or science, art or music—whenever you are working on a piece of nonfiction writing. It is going to really help you to know whether or not you are working your hardest at describing information in your writing, or if you are just settling for good enough." We show a chart with four columns and two rows, with the bottom row filled out, like the one from Lindsay's class of freshmen in central Illinois, as shown in Figure 4–1.

We explain how a micro-progression works, making sure to highlight the main purpose behind the day's work: to help students work at the higher level they are capable of, not just the level that comes easily to them. "So each of these columns repre-

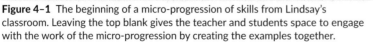

Figure 4–1 The beginning of a micro-progression of skills from Lindsay's classroom. Leaving the top blank gives the teacher and students space to engage with the work of the micro-progression by creating the examples together.

sents a different level of work. The first one is like a simpler level of work. And then the last one here is like an exceedingly complex level of work. And here is the thing: I made this especially for you because I know that every single one of you can already do at *least* the third level of work here. But sometimes you *don't*, because you kind of think it's good enough to do the first level all of the time. Today that can stop. Today I want to be sure you know exactly how hard you can work on your writing and I want to help you get there as often as possible."

We have the class take out their writing notebooks and pens. As we begin making the models for each level of the micro-progression, we want to be sure to get our students involved in the process, while staying aware of timing and the need for kids to feel confident when they walk away from the lesson. To that end, we begin by simply jotting down the first example, because we know that the entire class can achieve that level of work pretty easily. We pick a topic that the class knows well. In Lindsay's case, it was the topic she had been writing about for awhile in front of her class—her abilities at left defense in soccer. The class knew lots about her topic because she shared many stories and information about this personal topic of expertise. When teaching this lesson, Lindsay said, "So you all know about how much I know, and care, about good soccer defense. You have watched me write about my skills at defense, and how important I think the position is, and why. I want to show you now how I can use this micro-progression to be sure I've done my best writing as I work. For example, if I were working on this first level, my writing would sound something like this: 'I'm really good at left defense in soccer.' But I know I can do better than that. So I could also think about this second level. . . .'"

As we move up the levels of the micro-progression, we want the kids to become increasingly active, while not completely removing their support. To that end, when working on the second level of the micro-progression, often we demonstrate, thinking aloud our process, narrating exactly how we rewrite the first level to arrive at an improved second level. Then, for the third level, we ask the class to work together with us, calling out ideas for improving the second level, deciding which new lines actually meet the criteria of the third level until we have hit the mark. For the final level, we put kids in small groups of three or four to create more independence, making sure to coach as many groups as we can as they work. We curate the best lines from the different groups to arrive at the fourth level. The finished product, then, is something the kids have watched grow, and have co-authored, right before their eyes (see Figure 4–2 on page 58).

When we are done, we compliment the class on their hard work and say, "I knew you could do this. So here's the deal. Now that we know how hard you can work on your writing when you really try, you have to continue to try, a lot of the time. I'm not saying you *always* should be at the highest level, but you definitely shouldn't be at the lowest that often, because you can see how much better you can do.

"Can you, right now, talk to your partner about what level of description and elaboration you feel most comfortable with, and what level you'd like to try more often when you write? You might say, 'I'm super comfortable with the second level, and I'm really ready to write at level three more often.' And don't forget to tell your partner *why* you think you're

| I'M REALLY GOOD AT LEFT DEFENSE IN SOCCER. | I HAVE THE TECHNICAL SKILLS IT TAKES TO EXCEL IN THE POSITION OF LEFT DEFENSE IN SOCCER. | PEOPLE THINK GOALIES OR FORWARDS ARE THE MOST IMPORTANT PLAYER ON THE SOCCER FIELD. I HAVE THE TECHNICAL SKILL IT TAKES TO EXCEL IN THE POSITION OF LEFT DEFENSE. FOR EXAMPLE, YOU NEED TO MOVE QUICKLY TO ANTICIPATE A STRIKER'S FOOTWORK AND BLOCK THE DANGEROUS SHOT. | PEOPLE THINK GOALIES OR FORWARDS ARE THE MOST IMPORTANT PLAYER ON THE SOCCER FIELD. I HAVE THE TECHNICAL SKILL IT TAKES TO EXCEL IN THE POSITION OF LEFT DEFENSE. FOR EXAMPLE, YOU NEED TO MOVE QUICKLY TO ANTICIPATE A STRIKER'S FOOTWORK AND BLOCK THE DANGEROUS SHOT. BEING ABLE TO STOP A SHOT FROM A RIGHT FORWARD MAKES YOU LIKE A SUPERMAN STEPPING IN FRONT OF A SPEEDING TRAIN; EVERYONE IS WATCHING AND NERVOUS, BUT THERE YOU ARE, BLOCKING THE SHOT AND RETURNING EVERYONE TO SAFETY. |
| NAME IT. ADD A WORD OR TWO TO DESCRIBE IT. | DESCRIBE IT WITH THE **BEST** WORDS YOU CAN FIND. | *TRY* TO DESCRIBE IT FROM A COUPLE OF DIFFERENT ANGLES OR BY INCLUDING SOME SUBCATEGORIES OR PARTS. | USE AN ANECDOTE OR METAPHOR TO FURTHER DESCRIBE IT. |

Figure 4–2 The Finished Micro-progression for Lindsay's Class

nership still underestimating the level of work they could try, either from lack of confidence or motivation, we gently push, saying, "Sometimes coaches put you in the game when you don't think you're ready. Like, you might not feel like a starter player, but your coach looks at you with confidence and drive and puts you in the game because she knows you can do it. This is one of those moments; I'm coaching you to get into a game

ready! You might say, 'I'm ready to write at level three more often because I know a ton about my topic and I know I can pack more information into my sentences.'"

As the class begins talking, we move from partnership to partnership, encouraging kids to help each other set goals.

We ask some students to jot down the level they want to aim for that week, while we encourage others to mark specific places in their writing where they could try higher-level work. When we notice a part-

of higher-level work. You may have doubts, but I have total confidence that you are ready. Let's try for this next level and I'll check in with you to see how it's going. You game?"

After this partnership goal setting, we send the students off to write, and we continue supporting students through individual conferences. During our conferences, we keep the micro-progression out front and center, pushing students to use it as a guide to work harder on their writing. Toward the end of the workshop, we bring the class back together. "I'm really proud of you right now. The way you worked today, trying to reach for the next level and then the next, is how writing workshop should feel more of the time."

Often students' performance is elevated, more rigorous, that day, and even the next. But soon we will have to use the micro-progression in a broader sense to help kids

Reminder: How to Make a Micro-progression

(For a more detailed look at how to make a micro-progression, refer to Chapter Two.)

STEP ONE: Decide on a skill to focus on based on student work.

STEP TWO: Develop the levels of criteria and write in kid-friendly language.

STEP THREE: Work with students to develop models.

see that they can work hard most of the time, not just when describing something in a nonfiction text. To help transfer the rigorous work of this day across all of their days, we try these moves:

- Whenever the class is working on nonfiction writing, or talking about information, make sure to point to the micro-progression as a reference. Do this during writing workshop and in other subjects, like social studies, math, or science, collaborating with colleagues when possible.
- Make new micro-progressions when necessary.
- Build in time for reflection each week, encouraging partners to use the newly built micro-progressions to set goals and assess their progress. Coach students to create *I can* statements by pairing the phrase *I can* next to their level descriptors. Students can then go back into their work to try for those goals.
- When appropriate, ask groups of students to try their hand at making their own micro-progressions. Brainstorm most of the skill-level criteria with the students and experiment with leaving out one level of description so students describe the missing description by leaning on what they know about the skill. Ask students to make their own models. This provides support for students to independently think about the different levels of skill.

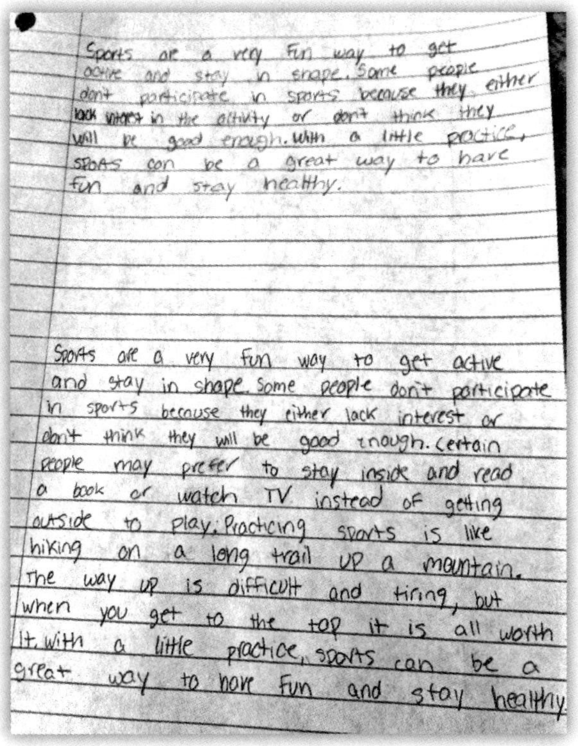
Sports are a very fun way to get active and stay in shape. Some people don't participate in sports because they either lack interest in the activity or don't think they will be good enough. With a little practice, sports can be a great way to have fun and stay healthy.

Sports are a very fun way to get active and stay in shape. Some people don't participate in sports because they either lack interest or don't think they will be good enough. Certain people may prefer to stay inside and read a book or watch TV instead of getting outside to play. Practicing sports is like hiking on a long trail up a mountain. The way up is difficult and tiring, but when you get to the top it is all worth it. With a little practice, sports can be a great way to have fun and stay healthy

Figure 4–3 Owen's revised nonfiction writing. The top piece is his original work. The bottom piece is the work after using a micro-progression.

☼ During conferences and small-group lessons, be sure to use the language of the micro-progressions. Ask students what level they feel they are working on and whether they could bump it up a notch. When ready, draft quick micro-progressions with kids when forecasting their next steps to be sure that they are being pushed.

☼ Create opportunities for students to celebrate growth in the form of personal testimonies. Students can share *before* and *after* examples of their work with a small group, saying, "I used to . . . but now I . . .," as a way to celebrate their growth, and motivation.

We know that our work is effective when we see students pushing themselves—like Owen, a sixth-grader. He realized that by using the criteria and models on a similar nonfiction writing micro-progression, he could do much more with his nonfiction writing when first drafting a piece on the benefits of sports (see Figure 4–3).

How to Set Goals and Narrow Our Focus

Because this lesson is designed to help Lindsay's students work as hard as they can, we built a micro-progression that did not ask students to do more than they knew how to do. Instead, we built a micro-progression that inspired them to do the best possible work that was within their reach. To do this, we did the following.

1. First, we looked at student work and listened to student conversations when they were more teacher directed. That is, we focused on moments when students were responding to direct prompting. This angled listening allows the opportunity to see what students are capable of when guided directly.

2. Next, we compared this work with what students did when given less explicit direction. Here we saw that students tended to work less rigorously when describing and elaborating upon information in their writing. This, then, became a goal for the rigor in class; we set a goal for students to work harder on their *description* and *elaboration*.

3. Last, we created a range of criteria for students to use to improve the description and elaboration in their nonfiction writing. To do this, we wrote the lower levels of criteria based on what we saw students doing independently and the higher levels based on what we saw many students doing with coaching and adult encouragement. This way, students can clearly see how to reach their full potential when working on their own.

How to Assess Whether Students Are Working Hard (*and Whether the Teaching Tools Worked*)

In many ways, if you are using a micro-progression to push the rigor in your classroom, you will have already created the main tool for your assessment for how hard your kids are working: their work should start to match the higher levels of the micro-progression more often.

Your assessment of their hard work will undoubtedly prove to be more qualitative than quantitative. It will be subjective and anecdotal. Here are some ways you can get a "sense" that your class is working harder:

1. Ask students to reflect on their work, either in writing or talk. Ask them, in particular, to describe how they pushed themselves and how they overcame obstacles as they worked. Students who have used their tools successfully will be able to point to areas of growth specifically, using the language of the tools, as in: "Before my details were kind of boring, but now I can use more specific words to describe them, and it helps my reader see what I am talking about."

2. Try what Dick Allington calls "far observation" of your class and note the behaviors you see. Here are some of the behaviors that often indicate hard work:

    a. Students' heads and bodies are hunched over their work.

    b. They are looking around for helpful resources, or looking back in the book or notebook they are using.

    c. They are stopping and thinking along the way; pausing is a good thing.

    d. They are talking to a partner to get ideas for how to move forward.

3. Compare student work from earlier in the year, or unit, to work after you began focusing more explicitly on rigor. Has it improved? What changes do you see? Be sure to name these for the student, and allow time for a celebration.

Fostering a Culture of Rigor: Five Ways to Cultivate Intrinsic Motivation

Teaching tools help show students that they *can* work hard, but you may need to do some work helping them to *want to.* In their hallmark study on intrinsic motivations for learning, Thomas W. Malone and Mark R. Lepper (Snow and Farr 1987) identify concrete ways to make learning more internally rewarding. Here are five ways to stoke the fires of intrinsic motivation in students.

1. **Challenge:** There is a reason why video games get harder as you move up levels. Students feel more internally motivated when attaining a goal is possible but not totally certain. Make sure the tools you create give students a vision for a level of rigor that is within their reach but might take some work to get to.

2. **Curiosity:** Half the battle is getting everyone to pay attention. Students feel a greater sense of internal motivation when their curiosity is piqued. Create tools that are visually stimulating and engaging. Choose colors, icons, and designs that spark students' attention.

3. **Control:** We all like to feel in charge of our own fates. Internal motivation is raised when the learner feels in control. Co-create the tools. The empowerment fosters agency and control over their own learning.

4. **Cooperation and Competition:** No kid is an island. Students feel more internally motivated when they see they are not alone. Use tools in small groups. This way, students have opportunities to see their work in relation to their peers', as well as help others achieve higher levels of work.

5. **Recognition:** Flattery will get you everywhere. When students are recognized for their hard work or improvement, they are more likely to continue working hard. Make space for public celebrations of progress and achievement, such as a bulletin board that showcases growth, or a special time each day or week to "spotlight" kids working hard.

Nurturing these five ways when using teaching tools not only helps students develop the internal motivation to work more rigorously but also increases the chances they'll be able to release the scaffold of the tool.

Other Tools to Help Students Work Harder

Micro-progressions illuminate a path toward rigor. But there are other tools that can motivate students to work harder. Here are a few other ways you could use teaching tools to help your students become more rigorous in their work.

USE A DEMONSTRATION NOTEBOOK TO PUSH SMALL GROUPS TO TACKLE NEW AND CHALLENGING WORK

Micro-progressions clearly map out the path for students to perform more rigorous work. In the earlier micro-progression lesson, we chose levels of work that students *already knew how to do,* essentially. We knew students were capable of rigorous work but needed a visual push to do so. However, what if students could work harder but still need more explicit teaching first? Demonstration notebooks are the perfect tool to use when students need some assistance in learning the actual steps and strategies to work even harder.

Theresa Walter from Great Neck, New York, was teaching a book club unit in her eighth-grade class. She saw that one of her stronger clubs was ready to take a next step in their reading, to notice author's craft. Theresa felt in her gut that this club could go further, but she also knew that they hadn't been taught to notice author's craft before. So, in order to work harder and to reach more rigorous levels of reading, she would need a tool to clearly lead them into that work. They were already doing powerful thematic work in their book club talks. Here is how Theresa pushed them further:

1. First, she began a demonstration notebook page with an example of what some of the club's talk and writing had sounded like so far—the 'before,' or the good work she wanted to make even better. Her example centered on a class text that she had read aloud earlier so that the club would be familiar with the text.

2. Then, she chose a few strategies that she thought this club could use to help them think more rigorously about their books, in this case, by thinking about the author's craft.

3. Next, she stacked blank sticky notes at the bottom of the page to create some repeatable demonstration space so that she could show this club, and any other students who could use this push, how these strategies ticked—essentially, how it felt and sounded to do this level of work (see Figure 4–4).

4. Last, she pulled the group of students together and explained the reason behind this lesson. Theresa told them she believed they were ready for the next level of thinking in their book club books, and that she wanted to spend some time showing them the work they could begin today.

As Theresa taught her small-group lesson, she used a couple of different methods for teaching her students. First, she leaned on the method of *demonstration*. She used the sticky notes at the bottom of the page as a space to demonstrate her analysis of an author's craft (refer to Figure 4–4). She said, "So you four are already doing this great work here," as she pointed to the top of the page, "thinking about the themes in your books and what texts are teaching you. But when you want to go to the next level of work in your books, you can choose a scene where this theme feels really important, and then you can look for some moves that the author may have made to reveal or highlight that theme. I listed

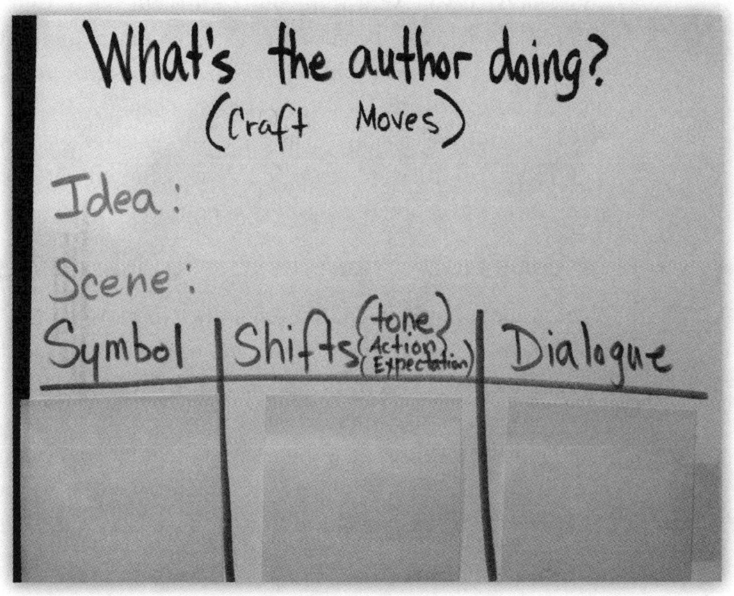

Figure 4–4 Theresa's Example of a Demonstration Notebook Page Used for Noticing Author's Craft

a few here, and I'm going to show you how I think about this in our read-aloud, *The Knife of Never Letting Go*, by Patrick Ness. Watch how I do this because you are going to try it next." Theresa then demonstrated her thinking about the craft in one scene of the text.

She said, "So at the start I was thinking about the ideas and themes of the text. I have been thinking that this book is about trust. But I want to get better at thinking about how an author's craft can be a spotlight for theme. So next I choose a scene that is a big deal for the issue of trust . . . like the scene where Todd is not sure whether to believe what he is hearing about Viola here." She flipped to a scene in the book. "And then I can read that scene looking for some of the things I know authors do to craft their writing, moves that I know sometimes help illuminate the themes in a book. Hmm. I could look for shifts in tone, literary devices, or maybe a symbol. Oh! A symbol! I see here in the scene that Manchee the dog keeps trying to get Todd's attention. And Manchee is, like, the most trusting being ever. If I think about Manchee as a symbol, I guess he would be a symbol of trust. Maybe Manchee is a symbol for what it looks like to be trusting. Let me write that on the sticky note here." Theresa jotted down her thinking on the sticky in the notebook. "See what I did? I picked a scene that went with my thinking, looked for some author's craft, and then thought a bit about how that craft might fit with the theme I am considering."

Then, when her demonstration was over, Theresa handed each kid a sticky note and asked them to try that same work on a scene from their book. As the club worked, Theresa moved from student to student, coaching their thinking. Her coaching matched what each student needed, ranging from helping them understand the terms she used, to articulating exactly what they were noticing in their text, to revising their thinking in the moment.

As the lesson ended she said, "So as you can see, this work is hard!" The kids nodded. "We are going to keep working on this as the unit goes on. Right now, can you take a few notes on what you want to be on the lookout for in your books from my demonstration notebook? And we will come together again to work on this page in a couple of days, after you have had a chance to practice. The point is that you keep trying, and work hard, not that it works perfectly for you right away, okay?"

If micro-progressions help kids work harder by showing them clear examples of high-level work they are ready for, demonstration notebooks create rigor by introducing students to the concrete steps, ways, or examples to begin challenging work with you.

USE CHARTS TO SPOTLIGHT THE STEPS TO HIGHER LEVELS OF WORK

If we want to teach a child to clean her room rigorously, we could, as outlined in this chapter, show her a micro-progression of clean rooms and help her to choose what level of cleanliness she is going to shoot for. Or, if we think she doesn't know how to clean her room, we can demonstrate cleaning a room with her so she can see how to do it. But at some point we will want to be able to create a shorthand method for her to remember what it means to be a rigorous room cleaner without us having to do quite so much work (work that may be necessary at first). Chances are that, at this point, we would say to her,

"Okay, time to clean your room. First, put away your toys; then, wipe down the surfaces. Finally, be sure to vacuum—and don't forget the corners!"

Once students have an awareness of rigorous work, charts are powerful reminders. Brianna Friedman Parlitsis, a literacy consultant, worked with a third-grade class across a unit on how to read fluently, with confidence and power. The class was ready to independently tackle this goal. So, she created a chart that helped kids check in on whether they were working on their fluency to their fullest potential. Here is how she went about it:

1. Brianna reviewed prior fluency lessons and picked three of the more challenging lessons that would lift the level of students' performance the highest.

2. She made a chart detailing the skill she wanted kids to work harder on (in this case, fluency) and used that skill as the heading of the chart. Then, she listed the lessons she picked as ways students could work on that skill more rigorously. She listed these underneath the heading.

3. Then she introduced the chart to students as a way for them to make sure they were reaching for challenging ways to do their best, most rigorous work as they read.

As students practiced reading their books aloud in partnerships, Brianna made sure to nudge readers to use the chart to help them achieve their highest level of work. Over the next few days, students added steps and tips to the chart as they worked, co-creating the ways that they could push themselves to work harder on their fluency in reading. The chart became a communal artifact, helping students to see the way toward more rigorous work (see Figure 4–5).

Figure 4–5 Charts can be cheerleaders for students to help them work harder. They provide encouragement, inspiring them to work to their highest potential.

USE BOOKMARKS TO SET PERSONAL GOALS FOR RIGOR

Rigor is relative. It's important to honor the fact that rigor looks different from classroom to classroom and from kid to kid. What is simply a breeze for one student is a mountain of difficulty for the other. We miss the mark if we only talk about rigor as a monolithic, static thing. If we lay out one goal for a class and only award those who get there first, we celebrate those who get there the quickest. But the journey of rigor comes in all sorts of paces—some slower, some faster. If we choose to prioritize the journey, and not just the destination, of rigor, then there are times we need to empower students with their own individual plan for how to work rigorously and at what pace. Bookmarks can help.

Worried about conventions, Kristen Warren, an eighth-grade teacher at MS 51 in Brooklyn, New York, embarked on a journey of teaching grammar, leaning on texts like *The Power of Grammar* (Ehrenworth and Vinton 2005) and *Catching Up on Conventions* (Francois and Zonana 2009). As she moved forward in the year, Kristen knew she wanted her kids to keep working hard on their editing conventions, but she didn't want to keep spending tons of class time enforcing and reinforcing the work. So she had her class make bookmarks for themselves to hold them to the high level of conventions work that she knew they could attain. Here's how she did it:

1. First, Kristen had her class look over their old work to find their most common convention errors. They worked with partners and she conferred with groups to help them identify their hot spots for conventions.

2. Then, she gave students some class time to make bookmarks for themselves that reminded them to be wary of their convention trouble spots, including examples of the correct usage. Kristen showed her (enlarged and annotated) bookmark first, to help them get ideas. (Refer to the "Companion Resources" section of the *DIY Literacy* page on www.Heinemann.com to see all of the figues in this book in color.)

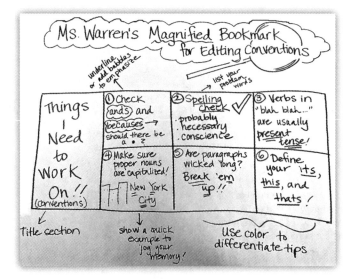

3. Finally, she had her students go back into their current writing, bookmarks
    in hand, to look for places where they could tighten their convention usage.
    To help her class stay focused and clear about the steps she took to make her
    bookmark, Kristen also devised a quick process chart. (To save chart paper, and
    because it was going to be a one-day chart, Kristen drafted it on plain typing
    paper and put it on her document camera.)

As the days went on, Kristen reminded her class to take their bookmarks out before
they began writing, and said, "Remember, anytime we are working hard on our writing, we
are trying to write in clear and powerful ways. Your bookmarks can help you to be sure you
are working hard on your editing work anytime you write."

Knowing the Way:
When Will They Be Ready to Give Up the Teaching Tool?

At first, students might see climbing the levels of a skill micro-progression as something
they do for you, or for a grade. But the ultimate goal is for students to work rigorously
for themselves. Students will not need as much support from us to work hard when they
exhibit a desire to roll their sleeves up and get to work without us coaching, pushing, or
begging them to. You'll know a student is ready to give up the teaching tool when he or

Quick Tip for Going Digital

It is especially helpful for students to be part of the process of making a teaching tool. First, creating something together helps demystify the process of how something is made. We, as humans, crave process. Just look at all of the wildly popular cooking or home improvement shows now—we love to watch something be created out of nothing! Demonstrating the process of creating a bookmark, for example, helps students see the steps involved in building it, rather than just seeing the end product. Watching the process of something being made increases the likelihood that students can replicate the process on their own, which is critical to their independence.

Secondly, we feel more ownership of things we've watched being created—the house you watched your grandfather build or the old bike you helped your cousin fix. When students watch a tool be created from scratch, the act of watching creates a memory and helps kids say, "I was there when that was made!"

To trap this in-the-moment feeling use a whiteboard program, like ShowMe Interactive Whiteboard or Educreations Interactive Whiteboard, to record the making of a teaching tool. Applications like these allow you to capture the creation of a tool in real time, recording the steps of how something is made as well as commentary as you're making it. And these platforms are easily passed to the hands of the students, where they can create their own recordings of tool-making to remind themselves of the process or to teach others.

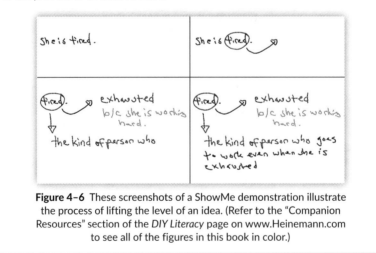

Figure 4-6 These screenshots of a ShowMe demonstration illustrate the process of lifting the level of an idea. (Refer to the "Companion Resources" section of the *DIY Literacy* page on www.Heinemann.com to see all of the figures in this book in color.)

she has created a sense of internal motivation to work more rigorously. Be on the lookout for these three signs:

1. **Working Overtime:** Just as an artist will log long hours in the studio working hard on a debut album, a student will devote time and energy when motivated to work hard. Notice those students who arrive early to class or stay late into

recess working on their writing. And pay extra attention to students spending periods of time working on a small section of their reading. Students generating their own steam while working for long periods of time generally can work without the teaching tool front and center.

2. **Reflections on Growth:** Listen for students reflecting on their growth as a reader or writer. Phrases like, "I've been really working on . . .," "I'm working to figure out . . .," "I keep thinking about . . .," "Something I've learned . . .," and "I'm trying something new . . ." indicate the process of learning, not just the completion of an assignment. Sound bites like these likely indicate the student has developed a drive to tackle his or her own learning projects. They are beginning to see their own trajectory of learning and can work independently of a teaching tool.

3. **Service for Others:** Students motivated to work hard will often show signs of wanting to be in the driver's seat. Locate the kids who show interest in making their own teaching tools, give tips to classmates, or could lead a teaching seminar on a topic they've been studying. Those types of "the-student-becomes-the-teacher" moments indicate signs of readiness in graduating from a teaching tool.

In Closing

Rigor has at least two components: (1) the difficulty of the task at hand and (2) the persistence and dedication of the students working toward that task. Without this second layer it won't matter how advanced our instruction is or isn't; if the kids aren't working hard, there is no rigor. As Carl Anderson reminds us when he speaks about conferring with students, if we are tired after a class and the kids are rested and relaxed, having not done that much, there is something off. One way to help your students work harder is to make sure they know exactly what it means, and what it looks like, and how to reach for high performance. You can take the mystery out of the vague command to work harder. You can show them the way.

Chapter Five

Just for You

Tailoring Teaching to Meet Students' Needs

Whenever you find yourself on the side of the majority, it is time to pause and reflect.
—Mark Twain

How Can I Help All of My Students Learn What *They* Need to Learn?

Every teacher knows the feeling of a Sunday night.

> It's Sunday, and you are planning for the week. You are in the middle of a unit, unsure where to go next. It seems like everyone is in a different place. Two groups of students are ready to be pushed to do higher-level work, but two other groups are struggling just to keep productive. You laugh after looking at what you planned to teach tomorrow. That lesson only fits one group! What can you teach your class that won't bore half the kids and confuse the rest? For a moment, you imagine writing three different lessons each day and teaching each one to the right group of students, but the thought of all that work feels, well, unsustainable at best, especially knowing that any given lesson might miss the mark. How can you make sure your teaching matches your kids?

We know that we need to differentiate our instruction. Ideally, while we devote some time to a whole-class lesson, we also use small-group instruction and individual conferences to tailor our instruction. This allows us to differentiate the work of the day, moving from kid to kid and group to group. This is probably an ideal solution to a classroom full of diverse learners. As Carol Ann Tomlinson says in *The Differentiated Classroom,* "a great coach never achieves greatness for himself or his team by working to make all his players alike" (1999). Few disagree that when working with a whole class of students there is a need to differentiate.

However, for most of us, when we are completely honest with ourselves, a "but" can sometimes follow that statement. That "but" usually sounds something like this: "Yes, I know this to be true, that my students need more individualized instruction. I see it every day, kids or groups of kids who need more support or who are ready for the next thing. But, how do I keep that up every day in a way that doesn't mean I am up until eleven every night working?" Or, more frighteningly, "But, what happens when I *do* plan until eleven every night, and students *still* don't seem to be getting what they need?"

This sentiment is not resistance, or lack of energy or care. Instead, it's rooted in a desire to create a sustainable practice that meets kids' needs. When we find ways to differentiate our teaching that conserve our energy, we are able to do more than just deliver lessons. We are able to imbue our teaching with the best part of ourselves—our love for the kids, our sense of humor, our deep compassion for students and the world. But how is this kind of differentiation possible?

During an Iyengar yoga class, the instructor typically sets a theme for the day's practice, say, aligning and supporting joints. The teacher then studies his students, taking inventory of the variety of forms, abilities, and limitations in the class. Instead of designing individual mini-classes for all the different forms and abilities he notices, he offers different props to different practitioners. One student might get two folded blankets to boost herself higher while sitting, easing the opening of the hips. Another might get two blocks to lean on so as to not collapse his side body while in triangle pose. Yet another student might get a rope to use while stretching her arms up toward the sky, preventing an overextension of her elbows. The yoga teacher uses tools to meet each student where he or she is, allowing each to gain full access to the goal of the class.

The teacher did not make each block or belt for each student in each new class. Nor did he hold students up himself when they needed support. Instead, during the preparation for his teaching, he invested time gathering the right tools and learning how to use them. In addition to gathering a collection of tools, he learned to see what students need in the moment of their practice and how to use the different tools in all the right ways. All of this work pays off by creating a sustainable system of truly individualized instruction in the midst of a thirty-person yoga class. By giving students the tools they need, the instructor is helping the students to differentiate for themselves. It is no longer necessary for him to observe and directly teach each student in order for them to make progress. While this is a benefit to the teacher in terms of managing a class—he does not need to be in multiple places at once—the most important benefit is to the students, who can now work at the level best for their practice without losing time waiting for the teacher and without the feeling that they must always be led through their own learning.

This is our hope for literacy instruction as well. Teaching tools won't make the work of differentiation effortless. But they make the work we put in have bigger payoffs, for us and for the kids.

Let's take a "type" of student as an example: the child ready for more. Whereas many days this child finds the lesson easy, and the conferences are few and far between (because she flies under the radar and completes most of the classwork with ease), class might feel more like this when teaching tools are at the ready:

1. The lesson itself is not the best fit for her; it's a little easy, but the teacher has made a chart (see Figure 5–4 later in this chapter for an example) that both captures the scope of the work for the unit and gives tips for how to push yourself which allows her to see where she could go next in her work.

2. She gets to work, using the chart from this day's lesson as well as other tools, like micro-progressions and bookmarks, to help her find her next steps.

3. When the teacher comes to work with her, he comes with a demonstration notebook that allows them to work on something challenging for her together, interactively (see Figure 5–1 for an example). She gets to practice this lesson once or twice before the teacher leaves her to try it on her own.

Teaching tools help us see the learning possibilities for all types of students. They meet kids where they are, guiding them to greater heights. Not only can tools give students something tangible to hold onto as they navigate their way through the curriculum, but they also give kids personalized learning footholds to find their next step along the way.

Demonstration Notebooks Help Tailor Teaching During Individual Conferences and Small-Group Work

In the lesson that follows, we focus specifically on how teaching tools can help our individualized instruction feel more effective. Here we spotlight a small-group lesson for students who are ready for the next level of work in writing dialogue in their stories.

After teaching a lesson on adding dialogue, we send the class off to work and begin our conferences and small groups. We pull our writers together, those students who are ready to be pushed beyond the work of the whole-class lesson. (We determined this by looking over their shoulders as they worked, noticing that the lesson was coming

Assessing the Situation: How Do I Know Whether Matching My Teaching to My Students' Needs Is the Issue?

You may need to focus on differentiating your teaching if:

1. You often struggle with what to teach your class next because there are so many different needs at any given moment.

2. A sizable percentage of your students exhibit signs of boredom or confusion by showing attitude or disdain, by acting out, or by seeming "lazy."

3. When you give an assessment, the range of performance in your classroom is very wide. This indicates that it will be challenging to meet your students' needs primarily through whole-class teaching.

Figure 5–1 Heather Burns' demonstration notebook page. The model story at the top is one that the students know well because the teacher has shared it with the class before. This way, the model serves as a communal, known text to revise during the lesson.

Reminder: How to Make a Demonstration Notebook

STEP ONE: Identify a group of students' current level or ability, and then write like that level at the top of the page.

STEP TWO: Find, develop, or choose a few strategies that might help. (See the bonus chapter for more on finding strategies.) Write these below Step One in bright colors.

STEP THREE: Create space for your demonstration with sticky notes.

easily to them.) In front of us is our demonstration notebook, a thick sketchbook filled with pages of writing demonstrations. We begin by framing the work ahead. "I pulled this small group because I couldn't help but notice that you were ready for the next level of thinking about dialogue in your stories. I wanted to be sure each of you had a chance to push yourself as writers today." We open up our notebook and show the students a page designed just for them and the teaching they were ready for. Figure 5–1 shows one made by Heather Burns at MS 223 in the Bronx for a similar small group.

"Okay, so after the lesson earlier today most of you have found plenty of places to add dialogue to your writing. I could see that that work came pretty easy to you, right? You all are ready for the next level of work. I'd like to study a bit of what makes dialogue even more powerful in books and stories. Check it out: right now your writing looks a lot like mine here."

We point to the top of the page and read the example aloud. Prior to the lesson, we drafted a few lines of sample writing that mirrored the level of these students' writing. "You see, you have dialogue, and you are even trying to make the dialogue sound kind of natural, like a person talking. That's awesome. But authors, when they write dialogue, do more than that. When authors write dialogue, they also try to make the dialogue reflect a character's emotions, to sound like the people feel. Writers also pay attention to the dialogue tags—the actions or inner thinking that come right after 'she said'—to add layers or nuance to their writing. And, you know, sometimes writers hold back and keep their characters from saying what they *really* mean in order to add tension."

We get our marker ready and signal to the blank sticky notes underneath each strategy on the notebook page. We know that, whenever possible, giving kids choice also gives them agency over their learning, so we ask, "Okay, which strategy do you want me to try first?" When the kids pause, we wait, wanting the students to actually look at the strategies and think about them for a second. Usually, one student will offer a possibility, hesitantly, as in, "Um, try the first one? About the emotions?"

When they do, we beam. "Great! Yes! I can take each line of dialogue and see if I can make it 'match' the emotion the character is feeling. Let me try that now." We begin writing on the sticky note underneath as we think aloud so that students can see the work transform.

The demonstration sounded similar to this example from Heather Burns' classroom: "Okay, the fact is, in this scene Adam and Victoria are super uncomfortable and nervous around each other because they had a big fight the night before. And Adam is still really angry, and Victoria's pride is hurt. So instead of Victoria just walking up and saying, 'Hey,' I think she would sound more interested, because she really wants to make things right. I think she would say, 'Hi, Adam,' using his name to get his attention. But then Adam would *totally* just say 'Hey' back, because he is so mad. Hmm, let me keep going." We jot down what we are saying on the sticky note, so that soon it looks like Heather's (see Figure 5–2).

After this quick modeling, we like to continue the work with another strategy. So we say, "Okay. So let's try one more. Let's try this second one together, using dialogue tags to add nuance. This means that we can add actions or thoughts for at least some of the things people say in a scene. Like this." We take a new sticky note and try the second strategy together. Leaning on Heather's example, the coaching sounds like, "I could take the first line here and add a small action from Victoria after she says 'Hi, Adam,' that could show how she is nervous and eager. Like . . . hmmm. I could write, '*Hi, Adam,*' *Victoria said, playing with her hair and looking him in the eye.* See that? It adds another layer to the dialogue."

After we have demonstrated, we want to give the kids a chance to try out the strategies on our model before they face the pressures of their own story. We say, "Now you try. Each of you take a sticky note." We hand out blank ones that were stacked underneath the

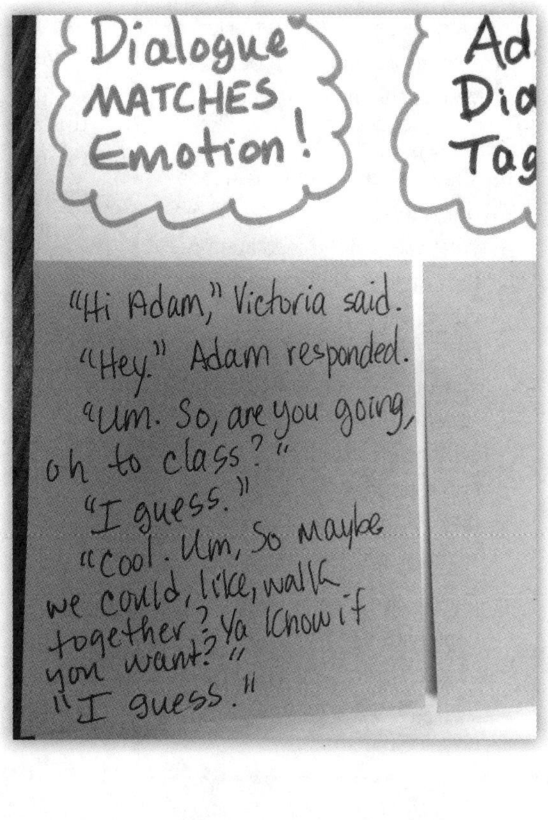

Figure 5–2 Heather Burns' revised model in a demonstration notebook page. By using sticky notes to work on, a teacher can use the demonstration notebook repeatedly over time.

How to Set Goals and Narrow Our Focus

To match our teaching to students' readiness, we have to do some prep work. We have to determine the range of skill levels in the classroom and then create tools that support students at those levels. To do this:

1. First, look at student work, particularly that of students who were generally above or below the level of the whole-class teaching. As we group similar pieces together, we ask, "What is the greatest need facing this writer/these writers right now?"

2. Next, with each pile of student work, reflect, "What's the lesson that might help this group of writers the most right now?"

3. Then, as a way to create strategies that meet the needs of these students, think about what the writers need and how they might go about doing that work. This way, each strategy has a **WHAT** and a **HOW**. For instance, "One way writers experiment with dialogue is by holding back what the characters say to each other." (See our bonus chapter for ways to develop these strategies.)

4. Finally, create tools like the demonstration notebook page to give students that you have targeted opportunities to practice the strategy.

one we demonstrated on. "Jot down a few actions or inner thoughts that could be added on to each line of dialogue that might add a layer to these characters, revealing more of what's going on for them. Give it a go." Then we wait, watching to see whether the kids can dive in and try. We know that if they can't, we can jump back in and demonstrate more. If students are able to attempt the work, we bring them together and ask them to share a bit.

We listen then to what students have worked on, coaching if need be, but mostly paying attention to the small leaps that show the strategies working, things like: "We thought you could add some actions like, 'her eyebrows were raised hopefully'" and "For the second line you could try, 'he mumbled a quick hello as he slammed his locker shut.'"

Whatever work our students have done, we want to congratulate them on their effort. We can always confer with a student or two who is still struggling. Ending the small group with a focus on the purpose of this work, we say, "Nice. So do you see how dialogue is not just about throwing in some 'he said,' 'she said' stuff? It's about using dialogue to reveal lots about these characters and this scene—all of the emotions and issues underneath the surface. It creates layers to your writing. You are ready for this work. Take a second now and decide what you will focus on today. Do you want to focus on making sure your dialogue matches the emotion of the scene, or do you want to jump into the dialogue tag work? Or do you think you can handle both?"

Having helped them set some goals for their work, we send the students off, reminding them that if they forget what to do they can always check out the demonstration notebook to remind them. (And we leave a sticky note with their names as a tab on the page so they can refer back to the lesson easily.)

Every time we teach a demonstration notebook lesson, we can't help but begin thinking of what other kids need help with. Often, we make a short list of these need trends, imagining gathering small groups of students around our notebook, and we continue to make pages. Off this particular lesson, for example, we specifically made pages for what you see in Figure 5–3.

As the year progresses, we want to keep up the work of filling our demonstration notebook with pages that will help teach kids at varying levels in our classroom. Soon we find ourselves leaning heavily on the demonstration notebook work as we plan units, being sure to think ahead to what pages we might need every step of the way to help push and support kids.

Figure 5–3 Examples of Demonstration Notebook Pages

TREND	DESCRIPTION OF DEMONSTRATION PAGE	EXAMPLE
Students need more support.	Make a page for kids still working to stretch out their scenes instead of summarizing them quickly.	
Students need more practice.	Make a page for strategy taught during the whole-class lesson, leaving extra room to practice together.	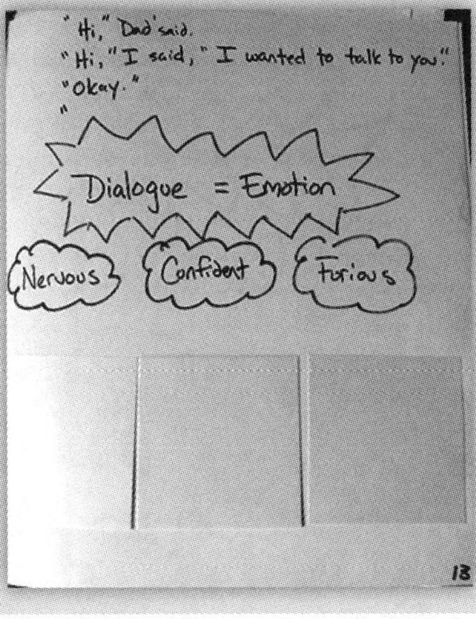

(continues)

How to Assess Whether Your Teaching Matches Your Students
(*and Whether the Teaching Tool Worked*)

The act of matching your teaching to your students requires by definition a consistent assessment of how things are going. Waiting to assess until the unit's end runs the risk of creating a mismatch between the unit's content and your students' needs. Here are a few ways you can assess in real time whether or not your teaching tools are hitting the mark.

Figure 5–3 (*continued*)

TREND	DESCRIPTION OF DEMONSTRATION PAGE	EXAMPLE
Students are ready for a challenge.	Make a page that explores how to show a person's complexity.	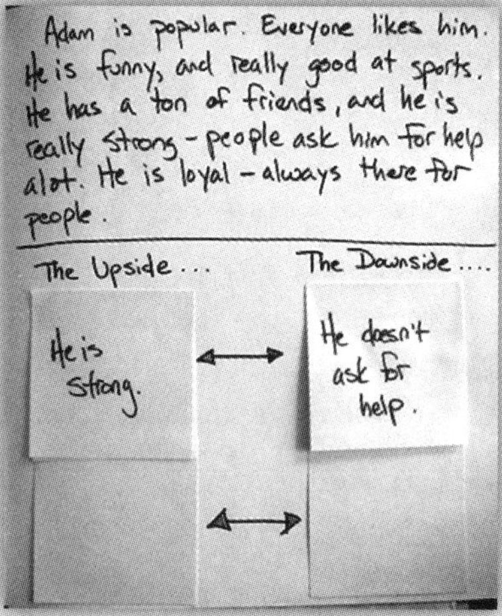 Adam is popular. Everyone likes him. He is funny, and really good at sports. He has a ton of friends, and he is really strong – people ask him for help alot. He is loyal – always there for people. The Upside... The Downside.... He is strong. He doesn't ask for help.
Students need grammar or mechanical support.	Make pages that show *before* and *after* examples of different rules, like punctuating dialogue or creating paragraph structures.	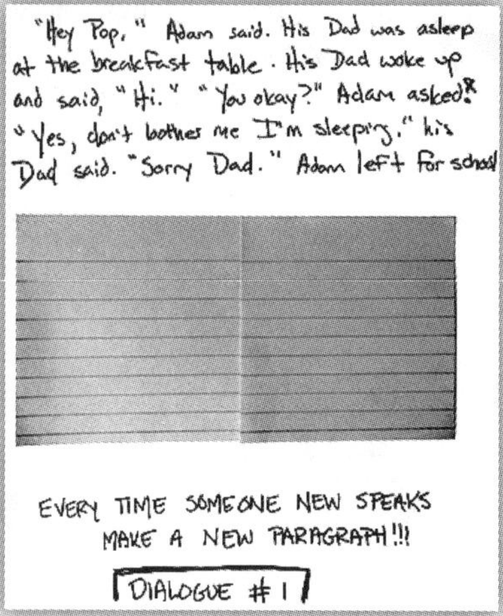 "Hey Pop," Adam said. His Dad was asleep at the breakfast table. His Dad woke up and said, "Hi." "You okay?" Adam asked. "Yes, don't bother me I'm sleeping." his Dad said. "Sorry Dad." Adam left for school EVERY TIME SOMEONE NEW SPEAKS MAKE A NEW PARAGRAPH!!! DIALOGUE #1

1. **Poll your class.** Create a digital survey, perhaps using Survey Monkey or a Google form, to quickly get a sense from your class whether they feel like the teaching is too hard, too easy, or just right. Or, of course, just ask them. Questions like, "Did this week's lessons push you?" or "Did you try or learn anything new this week?" or "Were there times you couldn't do what was asked of you?" can help to get a quick sense as to whether the curriculum is aligning with students.

2. **Look for growth.** As you look at student work or listen in on conversations, look for signs that students are learning new things. Often these signs are subtle; rare are the huge EUREKA! moments. Instead, look for one more line, a slightly more sophisticated thought, or an extra chapter read. These are signs that your students are responding to your teaching and moving forward.

3. **Look for struggle.** What "too tough" looks like might be somewhat subjective. Struggle is good, of course, but if your students are not able to make headway on a task without your help, that might be ineffectively difficult. Signs of unproductive struggle include acting out, spacing out, or defaulting to far easier work, such as a student retelling the book when he or she could be interpreting a theme.

4. **Look at engagement during lessons.** While we do not suggest that our teaching is only a good fit if our students are cheering and laughing at the end of our lessons, it is also true that if kids are bored much of the time, it may be because the teaching is too easy or out of their reach. If you notice lots of blank faces and glazed-over eyes, try asking your class how the work is feeling.

Other Tools to Help Match Teaching to Your Students

Demonstration notebooks are helpful, clear, and concrete tools to help you teach your students. "Making pages" to match what different students need allows all of your students to have access to teaching no matter where they are in their writing and reading lives. But there are other tools you can use to help all of your students learn. Here are a few ideas.

USE CHARTS TO RECORD A RANGE OF STRATEGIES FOR STUDENTS TO TRY

While charts are often used to help students remember what has been taught or to hold themselves to higher levels of performance, you can also use charts to help students troubleshoot their own work. This way, students can place themselves within the framework of your teaching, finding the right fit for their work that day. Creating an "If/Then" chart helps your students think through what *they* are ready for.

Anastasia, a fifth-grader, was feeling a little lost at how to begin her reading work after a lesson on summarizing nonfiction. The lesson "was good," but she "didn't really get it." But her teacher, Elayne Lipkin, a veteran teacher at PS 206, was busy conferring with another student. So she looked around. Elayne had made a chart with her class as the unit

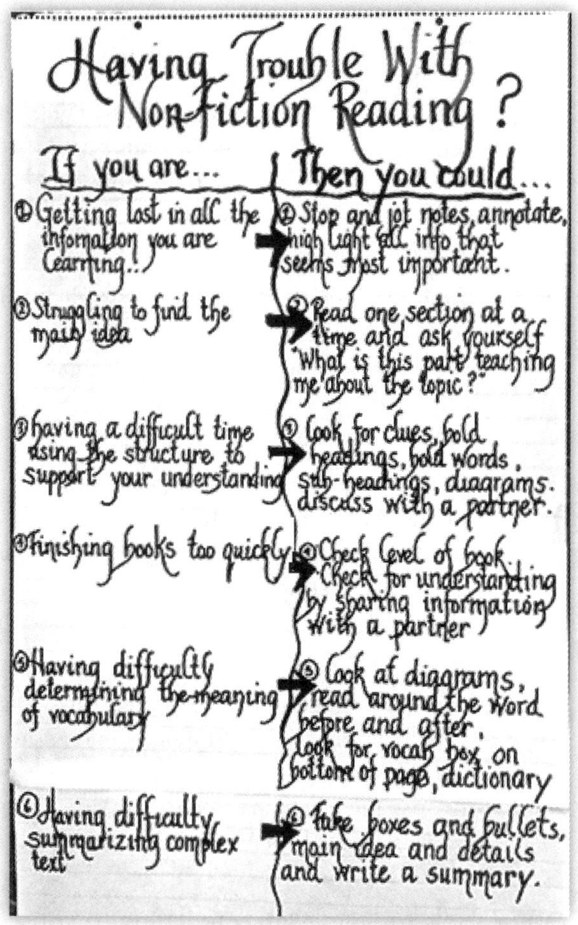

Figure 5–4 Elayne's Fifth-Grade "If/Then" Chart for a Nonfiction Reading Unit

began. Its columns were titled "If . . ./Then . . ." and it had several ways to keep busy working if anyone got stuck while working. Elayne asked the class to be sure to check in with the chart if they found themselves struggling, so Anastasia looked for her situation on the "If/Then" chart, and found it quickly (see Figure 5–4).

Anastasia saw that if she didn't get the summary lesson, she could use a simple outline structure to begin collecting main ideas and supporting details to help her get started. She knew how to do that! Using the chart, she found a way to get right to work.

To make this chart for her class, her teacher, Elayne, proceeded like this:

1. She looked across the scope of her unit and identified predictable problems kids might have when moving through the lessons. Making sure to focus on a variety of problems, she identified both simple and sophisticated problems kids might encounter.

2. She turned the predictable problems into scenarios. She filed these scenarios under a section of her chart labeled "If you are . . ." and made sure to write the scenarios in kid-friendly language.

3. Elayne imagined or recalled solutions or strategies that could be paired with each scenario. These became the "thens"—the ways students could tackle the problem they were facing. To be sure students could find the solutions independently, she leaned on familiar strategies, or strategies students could try on their own with some ease. This way, when students found the their problem on the chart, they had a clear road map to find a teaching solution.

When Elayne introduced this chart to her kids near the beginning of the unit, she said, "So during this unit, I am going to work really hard to teach you the lessons that I think will help you most. But I have to admit something to you: sometimes I will miss the mark. You will be sitting there, listening to me, thinking either, 'This is so easy, how boring,' or 'Oh my gosh, I don't know what she is talking about.' And that might happen on a day when I can't get to you in a conference, so we will have to have a plan for how you will be able to read deeply even when the teaching that day didn't work for you. Here is one way we can do that."

Charts can help students make a plan for themselves when we can't be there to find the right fit for them.

USE BOOKMARKS TO HELP STUDENTS CHOOSE THE STRATEGIES THAT WORK FOR THEM

Bookmarks are an ideal resource for students who need more individualized teaching. After all, kids make them based on what their goals are for their work, or what you have coached into and named as next steps. Bookmarks are truly individualized tools. It is quite possible that no two bookmarks look the same in your classroom.

In Anna Bennett's classroom at PS 59 in Manhattan, deep into an author study, she noticed that her class was a little all over the place. She realized she had been marching ahead in her teaching, offering her students a new lesson on studying authors each day. While she was giving her students a ton to think about and try, some were keeping pace with her easily while others were lagging far behind. So, she took a day to help her kids find themselves within all the teaching.

At this point in the unit, Anna had other visual tools displayed in her classroom that captured much of the previous teaching. There were charts of the strategies she had taught, and a micro-progression for thinking about authors the class had leaned on for the past week and a half. Today, she wanted her class to pause, look at what they had done, and set some goals for the future. Here is what she did to get ready:

1. Anna made sure that her charts and micro-progressions were visible to the class, since these tools would be a main source for the content of the bookmarks.

2. She made her own bookmark (see Figure 5–5) by selecting a few of the strategies she had taught, jotting them down on a slip of paper, and drawing a quick icon (if she could and if it seemed appropriate). Having students represent ideas and strategies in drawings, shapes, and icons helps them to understand and hold onto the work.

Figure 5–5 Anna's bookmark. Allowing students to engage with a teacher-made bookmark first helps them feel more confident when making their own bookmark.

Figure 5–6 A student practices using a teacher-made bookmark.

3. Anna chose to give her kids some time using her bookmark first, before they made their own. This allowed them to get a sense of how a bookmark works (see Figure 5–6).

4. She gathered materials for her students to make bookmarks themselves.

5. She thought ahead about which of her students might need a little support to get going; this did not necessarily mean the students who were "struggling" with the work. She thought about a wide range of students—some who needed support focusing, others who needed support lifting the level of their work, and a few who needed to set themselves up for a challenge. She made a plan to get to these kids first thing after her whole-class lesson.

The next day she said, "We have done some great work so far, but I realized last night that we could really use a minute or two to take stock of where we each are and think about where we want to go next. So today we are going to step back and think about which of the lessons I have taught you will really work for you."

She named, again, the steps she took to make her bookmark. For instance, she chose a few strategies that were going okay for her but that were not done with ease yet. She also pointed out how she chose one idea that she hadn't tried yet, just to challenge herself.

Then she sent the kids off to work, being sure to go first to the students she was worried about soon after the lesson.

The thing that struck us most about this lesson was the power of choice. Anna empowered her students with a sense of agency, an opportunity to take stock of all they were learning and then design their own mini learning plan. When students make their own action plans for learning, the plans are not identical, with a one-size-fits-all feel; instead, they are tailored for each student.

Bookmarks exert a gentle pressure on your students to make choices about what is working for them and what they want to achieve with their reading and writing.

CREATE A MICRO-PROGRESSION TO HELP STUDENTS STAY IN THEIR ZONE OF PROXIMAL DEVELOPMENT

When you are teaching a skill that is central to the work of your unit (say, inferring the main idea in nonfiction reading) and you know that your class will come to that skill from very different places, a micro-progression can help students to model themselves after a *level* of that skill. Micro-progressions help differentiate the work of a unit because no matter where a child is on the micro-progression of that skill, they can find themselves within the range of levels and take their next step.

We have found this to be helpful as we work, for example, on students' retelling of books. Often our whole-class lessons seem either too hard or too easy for many of the students. So we pause the sequence of whole-class minilessons and work on a micro-progression of retelling with the kids. We come into class with the lower portion of the micro-progression—the criteria for each level—already filled out. Prior to the lesson we:

1. Look at data—records on students, the jots from their reading, and our memory of conferences—and study the range of retelling we see in their work. In Anne Good's classroom in Beaverton, Oregon, for example, some kids are really working on just telling the main thing that happened in the beginning, middle, and end of the books they are reading. Others are starting to use character names and even fold in character traits and problems—inferences—into their retell. Others are getting ready to be able to retell by using a common narrative structure, like "Somebody . . . Wanted . . . But . . . So . . ." (Macon, Bewell, and Vogt 1991; Beers 2003).

2. Write out the micro-progression, leaving the top portion blank so that the class can work on writing the models together.

3. Imagine what some of the top models might say for each level using the current read-aloud text. We want to be ready to encourage students to create the best examples they can, so we rehearse a bit of what they might say before teaching.

The next morning, as the class gathers at the meeting area, we introduce the micro-progression and the different levels of retell we think the kids are ready for. We begin by saying that it is most important for each student to find their comfort level when retelling and then think about what they could try next. "I don't want to miss out on teaching

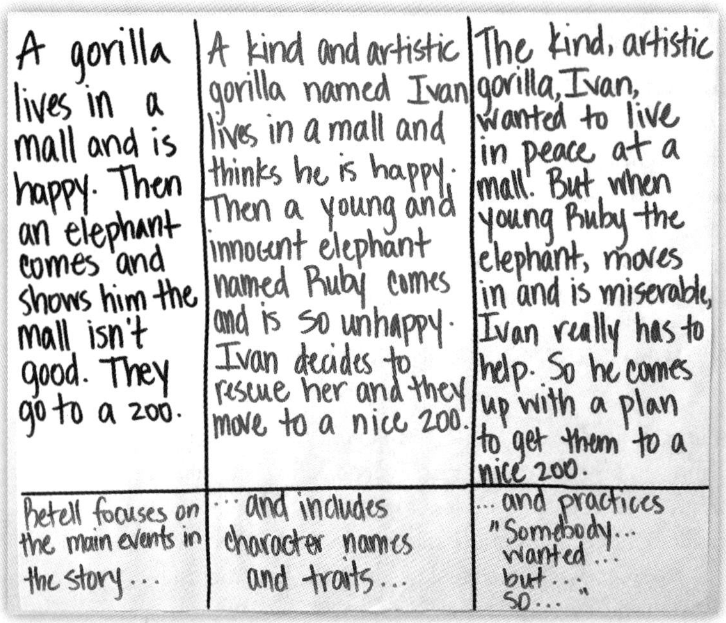

Figure 5–7 Anne's Retell Micro-progression Using Text from *The One and Only Ivan* by K. A. Applegate

A gorilla lives in a mall and is happy. Then an elephant comes and shows him the mall isn't good. They go to a zoo.

A kind and artistic gorilla named Ivan lives in a mall and thinks he is happy. Then a young and innocent elephant named Ruby comes and is so unhappy. Ivan decides to rescue her and they move to a nice zoo.

The kind, artistic gorilla, Ivan, wanted to live in peace at a mall. But when young Ruby the elephant, moves in and is miserable, Ivan really has to help. So he comes up with a plan to get them to a nice zoo.

Retell focuses on the main events in the story . . .

. . . and includes character names and traits . . .

. . . and practices "Somebody . . . wanted . . . but . . . so . . ."

any of you," we say. "I want to make sure each of you gets the right fit for your retelling work, and this micro-progression will help. Let's study the different levels of retelling that I'm seeing around the room and come up with some examples of each level together. We can use our read-aloud to help us do that work."

Knowing that the kids will benefit from a bit of demonstration first, we show them how we could create a retell of the read-aloud that matches the first set of criteria. Then, we have the class work together on writing an example for the second level, coaching and co-constructing that model as a class. For the last level, we have students work in groups, and we go to each group as they work and collect examples, fusing their work into a workable final example. Soon our class retell micro-progression looks like Anne's example, as shown in Figure 5–7.

Right before we send the kids off to work on their own books, we ask them to quickly name with their partner what level of work they feel they might reach for that day. As they talk with their partners, often we feel a sense of relief. Even if we can't get to every child that day, there is something in the room that can help them to work on what *they* are ready for.

Micro-progressions help students find where they are inside the curriculum, where they fall in their reading or writing skill level, and locate their area of readiness for future work.

Quick Tip for Going Digital

Matching teaching to students' needs takes a hefty amount of housekeeping. Stacks of writing notebooks, notes from student conferences, jots from different groups of kids—it's enough to make anyone's head spin! Despite our good intentions of differentiating, we can end up swimming in paperwork if we don't get the right organization system in place. Moving from stacks of notebooks and file folders to a digital system can help.

Evernote (see Figure 5–8) is an incredibly helpful app that allows you create digital notebooks for different subjects, topics, or students. For instance, you might have notebooks for different subjects ("Reading," "Writing," "Math") or for different units ("Argument Essay," "Nonfiction Reading") and so forth. You could also have separate notebooks for each of your students.

Evernote is highly flexible. Within each notebook, you can certainly type notes, but Evernote also allows you to insert photos (of student work, graphic organizers, etc.) or even recorded voice messages (of a student reading aloud, or your own observations). You can also "tag" each item so that you can easily find similar items no matter what student, class, or subject you've filed them in. All of these features allow you to track your students' progress across the marking period, unit, or year.

Taking notes digitally brings clarity to the ways you differentiate in the classroom; the information you need about your students is quite literally at your fingertips. At a glance, you can see what tips you tend to give students struggling with the work or students needing an extra boost. This way, as you work to match your teaching to your students, you won't have to reinvent the wheel. Everything you plan, all of the predictable problems you face, will be recorded in one accessible place.

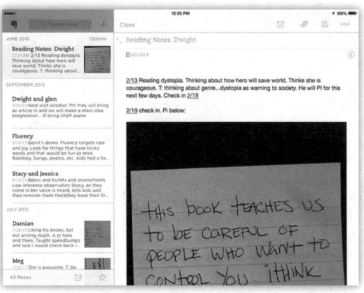

Figure 5–8 Screenshot of an Evernote conferring notebook.

Evernote, the Evernote Elephant logo, and REMEMBER EVERYTHING are trademarks of
Evernote Corporation and used under a license.

Knowing the Way:
When Will They Be Ready to Give Up the Teaching Tool?

In reality, you'll never be done differentiating for your students. They'll always be ready to be pushed to a new level, or need more support when trying something new or tricky. Teaching tools will always help them to reach for a new level of work, extending their reach from their place of readiness.

So here, the question is less "When will my kids no longer need teaching tools?" but more "When will I know that my kids have exhausted this particular tool and are ready for the next one?" To answer that question, you can look for:

1. **Automaticity:** Your students will not need a particular teaching tool anymore if they are able to do the work the tool supports automatically, especially when beginning the work. You see automaticity in their body language and demeanor; there is an ease to their work, as if it feels natural to them.

2. **Awareness:** Ask your students whether they feel ready to move on. Students as early as third grade will be able to identify whether or not they need a certain support while working. Babies know when they are ready to let go and stand on their own; your students will know when they are ready to give up a tool. Ask them.

3. **Agitation:** When students are ready for next steps, they will often show it in unseemly ways. Rare is the student who walks up to you and says, "I'm done with this level now; could you please offer me the next step?" Instead, they may act bored, irritated, goofy, or naughty. See these behaviors as signs of readiness for something easier or harder.

In Closing

Matching teaching to our students is no easy feat. After all, there are so many students, and only one of us! We are outnumbered. And while we might like to think that we can get to everyone every day (or every other day, or every week), the truth is that all too often we cannot. Sometimes we find ourselves running around the room, trying to touch base with every student. We are often hustling, trying to make quick connections and meet each child's needs. It helps to have an extension of ourselves that can support students when we can't be in all places at one time. Teaching tools offer students support and inspiration when we can't be by their side.

Chapter Six

Nuts and Bolts

*Tips for Making Teaching Tools
Effective and Engaging*

---

*Often it isn't the mountains ahead that wear you out,
it's the little pebble in your shoe.*
—Muhammad Ali

It's All in the Details: How to Make and Use Teaching Tools Effectively

For every grand production there are the behind-the-scenes players who manage all the details essential to the success of the performance. Without paying attention to these details—without the stagehands on Broadway, the traffic cops during rush hour, the cooks in the kitchen—the grand design doesn't shimmer as brightly or move as smoothly, and, in the worst case, it falls apart.

We see this in teaching, too. Sometimes the greatest lesson falls flat because, say, we've forgotten the colored pencils on the coffee table at home. Often what makes an extraordinary, abstract idea work is an ordinary, literal, physical *thing*. Perhaps if half of the class had been given a planning template, like an outline, they would have been able to begin writing and planning right away. Or, perhaps, a sorting game where students match text evidence with an author's claim would have gone that much better if those colored pencils had been available to hold their focus.

It's these tiny details that make the most of teaching tools, too. In the previous chapters, we outlined ways to use teaching tools to help realize the biggest hopes we have for students when creating learning experiences for them. We tethered each hope—memory, rigor, differentiation—to concrete, teaching-tool solutions in our dream of helping our students soar.

Over the years we have picked up a few tips and tricks when designing the details of teaching tools so that we could get the most out of them. We've learned from our mistakes, which included a chart with handwriting a bit too small and a micro-progression hung in a corner of the room with little student foot traffic. On the other hand, it isn't necessary to have perfect penmanship or a graphic arts degree to create powerful, effective teaching tools with your kids. Effective teaching tools come in many shapes and sizes. Some of the teachers who shared their work with us would identify themselves as artistic or visually proficient, but many more would not. However you identify, we hope that the tips that follow will help as you make, and use, your teaching tools.

In this chapter, we strive to troubleshoot the most common problems and pitfalls we have faced when making teaching tools for students. These tips are designed to help with the "pebbles in your shoe" that you may find on this journey. Removing these pebbles will lead to better, brighter, clearer teaching tools that help ease the way for our kids.

Problem: *My Students Are Not Responding (Anymore) to the Teaching Tools Around Them*

As anyone who has ever dated knows, connecting to another person is less about being perfect and more about chemistry. People don't click unless they are compatible. What works for one doesn't work for another. The same could be said for connecting your teaching tools to your students. The tools can be perfect—designed beautifully, completely standards-based, tailored to fit students' needs—and still not click with our kids. Similarly, students might start out using and loving a teaching tool, but over time might fall out of love. Here are some ways to keep the spark lit between your students and the teaching tools they need.

Use Pop Culture and Metaphors

Students have grown up immersed in popular culture. For every hour a student is in school, that student matches it with an hour of media. In 2010, an average sixth-grader spent more than $7\frac{1}{2}$ hours a day consuming media, a number most likely on the rise. Students live in a world of songs, games, shows, cultural events, and social platforms that we, as teachers, can tap into lightly as a way to nod at their media-rich lives. This nod, this act of engagement, helps our teaching feel even more relevant for students. And we argue that this engagement is critical for students when learning something difficult. When tackling something new or rigorous, kids (in fact, people of all ages) need fuel to keep them going and plugging away at the hard stuff. A cultural nod to their world—a light reference that's funny or familiar—can be just the thing to provide comfort and energy when facing something unknown and difficult on the journey.

POP CULTURE

Cracking open the window into popular culture can breathe life into curriculum. Referencing popular culture—whether it be something students are obsessed with or something they despise—offers kids a chance to lean into the work when they may have backed away. When it comes to pop culture, you might find yourself in one of two camps. Perhaps you're the person in your friend group who posts the latest viral video to your social media stream, knows what is trending on Twitter, has a teenager, and can sing along to the Billboard hits of the week. Or maybe you are closer to the person who feels a bit at sea—your teenager is grown and launched and you're not sure who the artists are on your granddaughter's iPod. Whichever way you lean, here are some concrete ways you can make inroads into students' popular cultural interests when building teaching tools.

☼ **Take a poll.** Conduct a survey of your students to learn about what they watch, listen to, or surf for on the Internet. Colleen Cruz, in her book *The Unstoppable Writing Teacher* (2015), suggests giving students a popular culture survey regularly, as trends in pop culture seemingly change overnight, She also wisely suggests that letting students take them anonymously allows for up-front honesty without the fear of embarrassment. (We've all turned down the volume on that new Taylor Swift song in the car at a red light, right?)

☼ **Look for snippets.** It's likely you are not totally interested in spending the entire weekend catching up on the oeuvre of EvanTube (a YouTube sensation). If hours of pop culture absorption are not your thing, do a few Internet searches that call up snippets or clips (one to three minutes long) of the shows, games, and songs your kids adore. Search for "EvanTube clips" or "Best EvanTube." This will get you a list of most watched, short clips of media, so that you can be in the know without devoting hours to researching online.

☼ **Find places to wink at the pop culture they love.** No one expects your classroom to become a shrine to Xbox. But it wouldn't hurt to layer in a few references here and there, and if it helps your class pay attention to the tools they need, isn't it worth it? For example, one teacher created a micro-progression that she "claimed" was given to her by Harry Styles, the lead singer of the band One Direction. She taped a picture of Mr. Styles to her micro-progression before hanging it up, with a dialogue bubble that said "Harry says. . . ." This playful wink was just the spark needed to draw students' eyes to the tool.

☼ **Search for parallels.** Be on the lookout for parallels in your teaching—cultural references that remind you of the work you are doing. Teaching a reading unit on character analysis? Isn't getting to know a character in a book kind of like getting to know your video game protagonist? Teaching a lesson on writing stamina? Playing a clip of a pop star talking about how grueling touring is might help make the point. A good pop culture parallel can be just the thing to pull a student's attention onto a teaching tool.

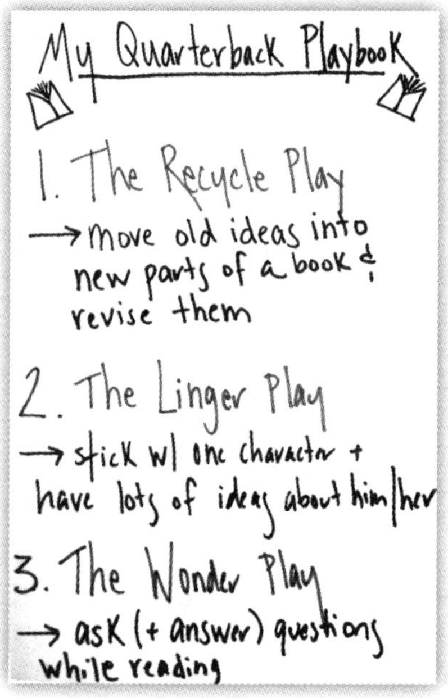

For instance, perhaps it's football season and you (or the diehard football fan in your life) notice the quarterback taking a look at his wrist before calling a play. Many quarterbacks keep a list of plays close so that they can make quick choices in the moment. These are moves the quarterback and the team know well and have practiced, but need a reminder for in the midst of a game.

You think, "Wouldn't it be helpful if kids had a bookmark reminding them of all the reading plays they know (but sometimes forget to use) when reading or writing?" Early in the year students can make their own "quarterback playbooks" in the form of bookmarks, with plays or "strategies" they know how to do well but just need a visual reminder of during reading or writing time. These playbook bookmarks could look like what is shown in Figure 6–1.

Figure 6–1 A bookmark in the style of a quarterback's playbook—a list of familiar reading "plays" or strategies to use when reading independently.

METAPHORS FOR LIFE

Of course, kids relate to things beyond popular culture. We can also seek out the connections between the strategies we teach and everyday life. Turning these connections into metaphors can help make teaching tools more relevant to students. Metaphors are memorable, and when the right one is used it creates relevance and impact. For example, when students revise a piece of writing, they have to channel a spirit of persistence and dedication, even in the face of challenges. Think for a moment: What other profession, hobby, or type of person channels a similar spirit? Firefighters, activists, and skateboarders might all come to mind. In Figure 6–2 we compare the essence of a writer knee deep in revision to the essence of a gamer. This metaphor-making allows students to feel like they know what we are talking about; it puts the work within reach.

To do this work yourself, take a step back from literacy and think a bit about what you are trying to teach your students. Literacy skills are often life skills, after all. When creating a metaphor for your teaching:

1. Think about what you are trying to teach.

2. Think about what might be a close example of that in real life.

3. Rehearse language to show the connection.

So, if you are making a tool for analyzing characters in books, consider doing this work in the context of real life. Where in life do we try to get to know other people? When in life do we analyze others—the choices they make, the things they say, how they act? At parties? At the cafeteria as we search for friends? At family dinners? The work of analyzing characters is much the same as analyzing people in life. We look for traits, strive to understand conflicting information, make judgments, and revise those judgments. There are parallels, whether we are reading a book or chatting beside a bowl of fruit punch. We can capitalize on these parallels when creating the metaphor linking the work inside and outside of the classroom.

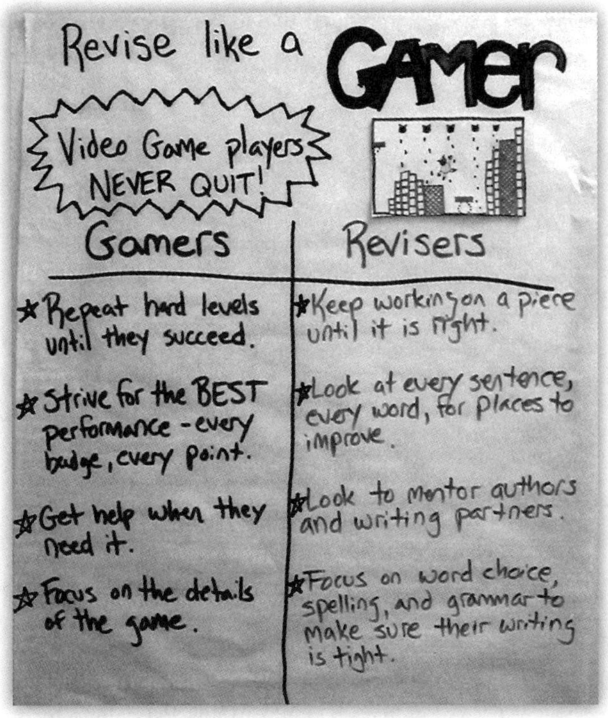

Use Kid-Friendly Language

Once upon a time, Kate went to a dinner party. Soon after arriving, while stuffing the first of many cheese slices and crackers in her mouth, she realized that almost everyone at the party was a scientist. At first this seemed delightful—how much she was going to learn! But soon this de-

Figure 6–2 A Repertoire Chart Using a Metaphor to Connect with Students

light turned to confusion when she realized that she couldn't really understand what anyone was talking about. The language they used was unfamiliar and technical. They talked at great lengths using words she could barely grasp.

The level of language we use matters, especially when communicating to students. If we use too much text on a teaching tool, or too much language that is too difficult to understand, students might be less apt to use it, especially independently. Similarly, if we use language that is too simple, that seems "babyish," then students might tune out and we'll miss an opportunity to support their language development.

Like the infamous Goldilocks, we are in search of language that is "just right" when we are creating or co-creating teaching tools. Here are some things to consider:

1. **Less is more.** Teaching tools tend to work best when they are more like haiku than lengthy prose. Search for simple, clear ways to say or explain things. Rehearse the explanation: if the description is lengthy, try saying it in fewer words and add it to the tool.

2. **Find the right level.** When writing on a teaching tool, make sure the class understands your choice of words. If your students know the word *obfuscate,*

great. If they don't, stick with *confuse*. Keeping language within reach for students is one way to support their independence when working with a teaching tool. The more likely they are to understand it, the more likely they are to use it.

3. **Teach a few new things.** While the above two points are true, it is also true that teaching tools *can* be a place to reinforce new words or language. Say you have been teaching your class Tier 2 words—high-frequency, highly functional words, like *describe* or *investigate*. Incorporating some of these newer words into a teaching tool is an effective way to reinforce your teaching, allowing students to use, practice, and hold onto new vocabulary. The trick is to return to tip #1 in this section: less is more. Ken Pransky reminds us that if students are taught eight to ten words a day, they will retain only two or three of them (2010). By prioritizing the new vocabulary you want students to focus on and by using those words in teaching tools, you layer another opportunity for practice and learning.

Mix It Up: Variety Is the Spice of Life

People in retail and sales say that one of the keys to successful sales is making sure an item is rotated around a brick-and-mortar store from time to time. It's a magic trick of sales—leave a shelf of Chia Pets alone for too long and they won't sell. But rotate them around the store and the products will move. Perhaps this is due to people falling into patterns as they shop, not seeing the newness when immersed in a totally familiar landscape. Or maybe there is something more mystical involved, some kind of energy around objects that shine brighter when attended to. Whatever the cause, the result is the same: if we want people to notice things, we have to change them up.

In your classroom, if you leave a chart or a micro-progression up all year long in the same place, it's likely that students will stop noticing it hanging there. It becomes background noise that is vague, indistinct, and uninteresting. Here are a few ways to maintain the energy of the space and keep the tools fresh and useful, inspired greatly by Marjorie Martinelli and Kristine Mraz's work in their book, *Smarter Charts K–2* (2012).

1. Consider the layout of your room as you plan an upcoming unit. Are there any charts you could move to the front that would be helpful? Could you switch where you hang your charts for different subjects or purposes?

2. If there is a tool that you will be using often with your class, consider making a new and improved version from time to time. Even if it is an exact replica of the old one, a fresh coat of marker can help make it pop.

3. Be sure to point to, reference, and generally make a big deal of any teaching tool you want the class to keep noticing. If we keep the tools alive, students will too.

While these tips are focused generally on the tools that get hung up on the classroom walls, such as charts and micro-progressions, the same theory can apply to demonstration notebooks and bookmarks as well. Change where you keep your demonstration notebook to help your students see it with fresh eyes. Help students see their bookmarks by continually referencing how kids might use them across the unit or year. Allow time for students to rebuild their bookmarks, creating new artifacts that represent their current learning goals. This kind of "upkeep" helps ensure that your teaching tools feel fresh and useful.

Incorporate Student Voice into the Teaching Tools

If students are shrugging at the sight of the beautiful micro-progression you made, perhaps it's time for them to roll up their sleeves and take more ownership of the work. Teaching tools that are created or co-created by students are almost always more accessible, engaging, and memorable than any you present fully formed. As your students decide what to put on the teaching tool, they engage with the material on a much deeper level than if they were simply listening or watching. As they draw icons themselves, the work solidifies.

Here are a few ways that students have created or co-created teaching tools in classrooms:

1. **You are the conductor.** Set the stage for the work of the teaching tool and have students make contributions in the moment. In many of the lessons in this book, the teacher sets up the work of the teaching tool, then has students talk to a partner or stop and quickly jot down ideas for another part of the tool (like when creating the model for a micro-progression or listing the strategies on a chart). Involving students in the creation of a tool creates student ownership while preserving the orchestration of the teacher.

2. **Everyone gives it a go.** When students make bookmarks, every kid in the class makes their own, thereby ensuring that they feel ownership over the work. You can create these same conditions for any teaching tool, however. Have students work in groups to make their own micro-progressions or charts. Have kids make demonstration notebook pages for work they have mastered. This way, your students are invested in the content and process of the tool before they have been asked to use it.

3. **Hire "experts."** As you notice students showing mastery of a skill, take them aside and ask them to create a tool, or part of a tool, for their classmates who are still on a journey of mastering that skill. Appointing teaching tool "experts" or "ambassadors" encourages students to learn the work deeper themselves, cultivates peer-to-peer learning, and allows them to discover the type of tool that works best for them. For instance, students can contribute a clear example of what a strategy looks like in action on a demonstration notebook page (see Figure 6–3 on page 94).

Figure 6-3 A demonstration notebook page shows student work serving as the example. Student work attached to a demonstration notebook page (instead of the more traditional "before and after" format we have highlighted in this book) allows other students to see an example of work that is clearly within reach.

Whether you choose to focus on pop culture, commit yourself to keeping the teaching tools in your classroom fresh, or concentrate on finding the perfect language for the tools you use, remember that classroom tools are only great if the kids use them. By staying aware of the role that teaching tools are playing in your classroom and your teaching, you can intervene when that micro-progression all the kids were using last week starts to fade from view.

Problem: *I Can't Organize All These Teaching Tools*

We recently worked with an outstanding teacher who had a knack for making gorgeous teaching tools. Her micro-progressions were lean and graceful; her charts made you grab your phone for a photo. She had effortless handwriting and an eye for design.

But when you walked into her classroom, a kind of chaos reigned. There were charts everywhere, hanging from every window frame, covering every inch of wall space. There were charts hanging on top of other charts. The beauty and helpfulness of the charts were getting lost in the fold. During a writing conference, Maggie and the teacher asked the student where she might find a chart to help with her essay writing. The student earnestly shrugged and gestured to a large area in the back of the classroom, "Over there, maybe?"

Creating an organizational system for your teaching tools and helping kids find and use them is equally as important as visually effective design.

Set Up Rooms to Be Teaching Tool–Friendly

When a museum curator plans an exhibit, he is working with many similar but different art pieces; he has many paintings to organize, many sculptures, and countless sketches. You are curating your classroom when deciding where to place different teaching tools.

Just as a curator must think about an organizing principle for hanging paintings across a museum, you must make some decisions about where the various kinds of tools will go in your room. Here are some things you might consider as you map out the hanging space in your room (also see Figure 6–4):

1. **Cluster the same subject's tools together.** When students know where to look for the charts for, say, reading, it is easier for them to quickly find what they need while they work. Select an area of your room for your reading tools, an area for writing, and a space for content-area tools as well, if applicable.

2. **Group the current unit's tools close to the front of the room or meeting area.** The teaching tools that fit your current unit are invaluable resources for your kids from day to day. Putting them close to most of your whole-class teaching (like close to your meeting area or at the front of the room) draws the students' eyes toward the most recent work. Organize extra copies of bookmarks in binders, or in a digital file on the computer, for quick printing or emailing, and in a handy, high-traffic area of the classroom. Place your demonstration notebook on a table for students to check out for the class period, just like a library book.

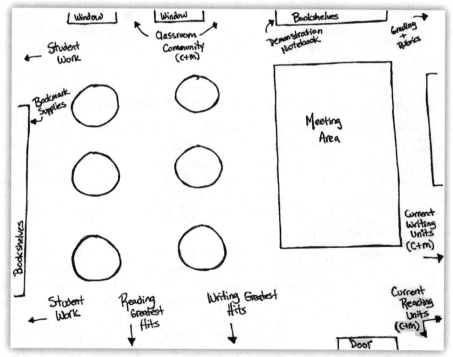

Figure 6–4 A classroom map showing where teaching tools could go. (**C+M** indicates charts and micro-progressions.) A quick map can give your room a logic that students follow when they are looking for something to help them.

3. **Quiz your kids on the layout.** No matter how flawless your organizational systems, your kids will probably need some encouragement to pay attention. It might help to create some in-the-moment pressure for your students to look around. When you start to feel that your class is no longer actively noticing the teaching tools around them, have an impromptu scavenger hunt for various tools. On slips of paper, write out tools for kids to look for. Here are a few examples of hints for a teaching-tool scavenger hunt:

   a. Look for a tool that could help you to come up with ideas for your writing.

   b. Where would you go to push your nonfiction reading?

   c. You worked hard and now you feel done, but there are twenty minutes left of independent work time. Which tools could help you stay productive?

4. **Offer students materials to make their own teaching tools.** Set up space in your classroom for markers, tape, sticky notes, and paper so that students can make their own teaching tools. Most often, kids will use these materials when making bookmarks, but there will be opportunities for groups to work on micro-progressions, to make a demonstration notebook page for a strategy they used beautifully, or to construct a chart for the class. By having materials at the ready, you are saying to your class, "You are a part of the making of these things. You are the co-creators."

Plan Times to Make Teaching Tools (Especially with Multiple Classes)

It is important to make teaching tools (or parts of them) in front of and with the help of students. In nearly every example presented so far, the classroom teacher has co-constructed at least parts of the tool with students: charts are made with student input, micro-progressions lean on students making the models, demonstration notebooks leave space for the kids to try some of the work. When students see something being created in front of them, with them, and by them, they have greater ownership over the tool and become more easily engaged.

But when you have multiple classes this can become a daunting and confusing proposition. How do you hang up one micro-progression if three classes have contributed to three different micro-progressions across the day? How do you afford all of that sticky chart paper? (That stuff isn't cheap!) Does your first class of the day get the awesome, interactive tool work and the rest of your classes just get a presentation of the earlier, already completed work?

It's not easy, and it won't be perfect, but you can create interactive, student-created teaching tools even when you have multiple classes of kids. Here are some options:

- ☼ Make a teaching tool with each class, and then take the greatest hits from each to make a master teaching tool to hang in your class.

- ☼ Pre-make the parts of the tool that won't change (like the lower sections of the micro-progression), and then tape pieces of copy paper to the parts that need to be interactive.

- ☼ Make tools with each class on smaller sheets of blank computer paper under a document camera, and then make a larger one to hang at the end of the day.

- ☼ Do the work digitally. Make the tools on your interactive whiteboard, saving each copy, and then cutting and pasting to make one version that all three classes can use.

- ☼ Make a tool ahead of time, but ask each class to add to it throughout the day.

Edit Teaching Tools Across Units and the Year

Pretty soon the real estate for teaching tools is going to be scarce regardless of how much you try to organize. As time goes on, and units end, you will have to be discerning about which tools you keep up long term. It stands to reason that you should only keep up the tools your kids will use. Have an editing eye; if you don't think that kids will actually use a tool when the unit is over, take it down. (Be sure to take a photo first to preserve the work!) A "Prompts to Push My Thinking" bookmark (see Figure 6–5), inspired by the essay work in *Boxes and Bullets: Personal and Persuasive Essays* by Lucy Calkins, Kelly Boland Hohne, and Cory Gillette (2013) will help students anytime they have to elaborate on a thought, and it should probably stay with them as a reference. A chart titled "Things to Look for in Dystopian Novels," however, may not stay as useful over time since it is so unit specific. When making decisions about which tools to hang onto and which ones to retire, consider the following:

- ☼ **The work on the horizon:** What work will students be doing in the near future? What kind of independent reading and writing skills would you like students to rely on often? Look around the room and choose the tools you think might help the class with that future work.

- ☼ **Poll the kids:** A great way to find out which teaching tools will be most helpful for students is to simply ask them. Have a conversation with your class. Ask them

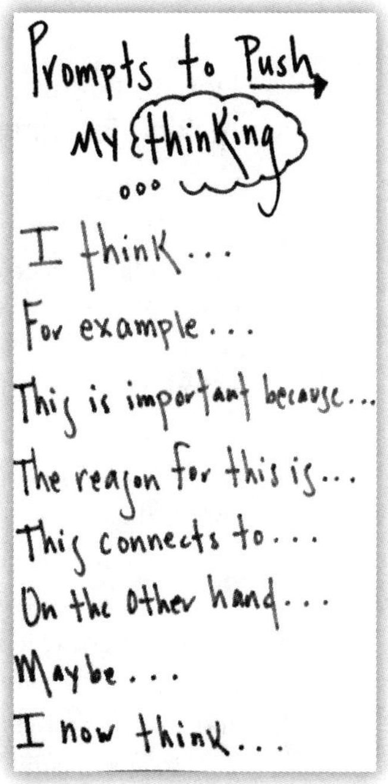

Prompts to Push
My Thinking
ooo
I think . . .
For example . . .
This is important because . . .
The reason for this is . . .
This connects to . . .
On the other hand . . .
Maybe . . .
I now think . . .

Figure 6-5 A bookmark (or chart) of prompts to help elaborate on a thought could be a powerful tool to keep alive across the year.

to choose which tools to keep up, which to retire, which need reinvention, and which can be consolidated into one.

☼ **Set priorities for the future:** There might be a tool that hasn't gotten a lot of use yet and you want to bring it to the forefront of kids' upcoming work. Maybe you taught one lesson on how to keep revising after you feel "done." You modeled making bookmarks to keep the engine of independent writing going, but notice students have stopped taking them out to use them. This is a great opportunity to "reboot" a forgotten tool—redesign it, create a new ritual around using it, and revise its content to make it more relevant. Be on the lookout for overlooked tools, and give them a second chance by referencing them or using them in new ways.

Problem: *I'm Not an Artist, at All*

You don't have to be an artist to make teaching tools that work. That being said, the way teaching tools look does matter. Kids need to be able to read them, and it definitely helps if they have some visual allure. Visual cues like icons and illustrations can really help some kids access information quickly. So, how can you make teaching tools artful and visually appealing if you are not an artist?

Let's break things down, and see if we can help bring out your inner O'Keefe.

How to Focus on the Design Elements That Matter Most When Making Teaching Tools

You are sitting in front of your blank piece of paper, marker in hand. You know what you want your tool to say. But you feel unsure where to begin (and don't want to waste that not-so-cheap piece of sticky poster paper). Here are a few things you could consider about the design of your teaching tool before you begin.

SPACE

White space is your friend when you are making any kind of tool. It is what allows the reader to breathe, to take in the information without getting overwhelmed. Research shows that white space around blocks of text helps readers understand what they are reading better by nearly 20 percent (Lin 2004). While there is a temptation to fill every part of your tool with valuable information, remember the ultimate goal: that students will use these teaching tools independently. They don't need to be encyclopedias of your teaching! If your tool becomes too crowded, it can become intimidating, even unfriendly, and students will be less likely to use it.

To give teaching tools breathing room, you might try these things:

☼ **Give yourself wide margins.** Make sure that there is some elbowroom on the left and the right sides of your chart or page. Don't start writing right at

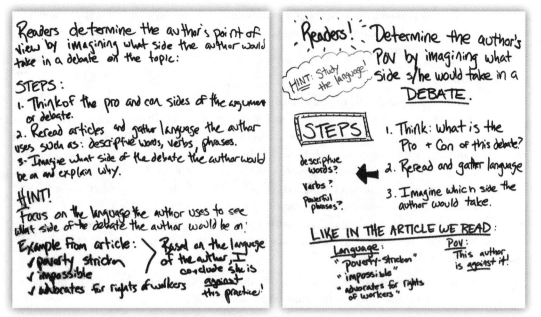

Figure 6–6 Do's and Don'ts of Designing Space: The chart on the left crams words together, making it difficult to see exactly what the work of the chart is. The chart on the right, however, has used white space and sections to help students read the chart more easily. (Refer to the "Companion Resources" section of the *DIY Literacy* page on www.Heinemann.com to see all of the figures in the book in color.)

the edge of the chart. Play around with the margins on your tool. Have the headline stretch to the edges but leave wide margins for the majority of text, or perhaps shift the margins around the tool as a way to create sections (see Figure 6–6). This way, the reader's eye can travel to the parts that are most important.

☼ **Write big.** In high school, you may have tried to get away with handing in a research paper in size 14 font, hoping that your teacher wouldn't notice (or maybe that was just us). While that ruse never seemed to work, now is your chance to unabashedly blow up your font size! Since teaching tools are meant to be used relatively quickly, larger lettering is usually the way to go. Make sure the letters are big enough that your kids will be able to read the tool, especially in the way it will be used. In other words, if your tool is going to be hanging on the wall, write the text big enough that the kid across the room can still read the words.

☼ **Separate sections.** Give attention to chunks of text by double-spacing between paragraphs, creating borders around different sections or headings, or being creative with the margins around different parts of your tool. Special design strategies can highlight different parts of your tool and make information pop. For example, enclosing text in a border brings attention to it, giving it more importance.

COLOR

One of the easiest ways to make teaching tools visually attractive and useful is to make smart choices about color. While it may seem frivolous, choosing a quick color scheme and a guiding color theory for your teaching tools will help students learn to use them more efficiently. For example, for one year in Kate's classroom, every chart she made had the title in black and then the strategies or procedures in rainbow colors, with the most important information up top in red. Over time her students knew what to expect and could locate the prioritized information quickly and with ease. Here are a few tips on color choices you can make as you design your teaching tools. (Refer to the "Companion Resources" section of the *DIY Literacy* entry on www.Heinemann.com to see all of the figures in this book in color.)

1. **Less is more.** In general, two or three colors are better than ten (except the previously mentioned rainbows, of course!).

2. **Try using shades of color.** Instead of deciding whether or not green goes with orange, try three different shades of blue.

3. **Use a consistent title color.** Try keeping the headings or titles of your tools all one color, like black or blue. This color choice provides clarity for your class so that when they see, for example, black, they know they're looking at the subject or title of the tool.

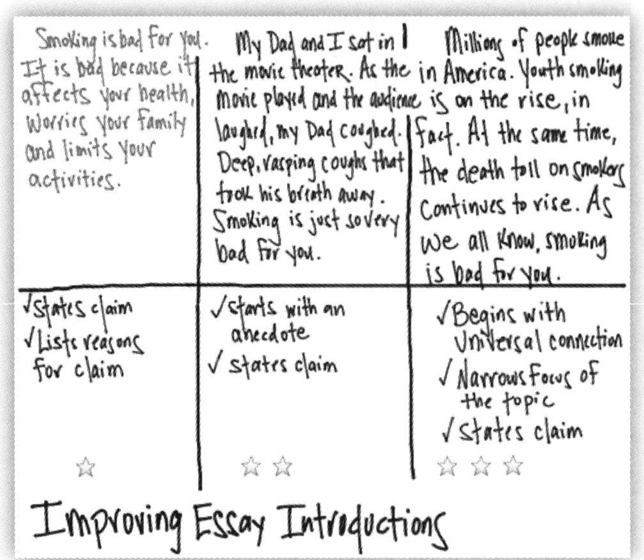

Figure 6–7 An Example of Thoughtful Color Choice: This micro-progression has a color plan—the criteria are all in one color, and the models on top use a similar color scheme. (Refer to the "Companion Resources" section of the *DIY Literacy* entry on www.Heinemann.com to see all of the figures in this book in color.)

4. **Brand with color.** What color are those McDon-
ald's arches again? Try branding certain parts of
your teaching with specific colors. For instance,
some teachers who were struggling with color
chose warm tones when making tools for their
reading class and cool tones for writing. Color
branding narrows the decision making for the
teacher and communicates clarity to students
because they can identify the subject at a glance.

How to Handle a Case of Sloppy Handwriting and Other Imperfections

This is the number one obstacle we have run across when
doing this work with teachers. Countless educators have
seen the need for charts, micro-progressions, and powerful
demonstration notebooks, only to be held back by their own
sloppy handwriting. And worse, it feels insurmountable; our
handwriting is our handwriting, after all. Sometimes even
when we slow down and concentrate, what comes out of our
Bic pen is still all but illegible.

This is a real obstacle to creating powerful teaching
tools. After all, kids have to be able to read them and use
them on their own. But there are some ways to make your
poor penmanship work for you (or at least help you work
around it). Here are a few strategies teachers have used to
combat the problem of the pen.

TRY USING ALL CAPS

For many people, simply writing in all capital letters helps
their handwriting become more legible. Research shows that
writing in capital letters slows down the readability of the
text, and for a teaching tool, that can help the reader. Writing in all caps provides a safety net for those of us whose
handwriting can fall every which way. Capital letters help
streamline the act of lettering and tidy up the tool.

TAKE YOUR TIME

Simply taking your time often helps handwriting improve.
Breathe. Visualize what you want the letters to look like before you start. Go slowly. Create a schedule for tool-making
so you don't find yourself in a rush—in the mornings over

Why Not Go 100% Digital?

You might be tempted to go
completely digital if you're not
feeling super confident about your
handwriting. Digitizing tools is a
surefire way to streamline and create
a cohesive look for your teaching
tools. Capitalizing on different fonts,
images, and formats can help solve
some of the design problems you may
face—but we hope you don't go 100%
digital.

Why keep some of the tools
handwritten? Handcrafting
tools creates engagement and
a personalized connection: a
handwritten thank-you card sure
beats an email, and a handwritten
note from your spouse left beside
the coffeemaker in the morning sure
beats a text message. Handwriting
experts agree: "There is an element of
dancing when we write, a melody in
the message, which adds emotion to
the text," argues Roland Jouvent, head
of adult psychiatry at Pitié-Salpêtrière
in Paris (Chemin 2014). "After all,
that's why emoticons were invented,
to restore a little emotion to text
messages." So even with all the digital
access at our fingertips, we still argue
for the handwritten micro-progression
that is without a doubt made by you.
After all, writing is a direct window
into our personality. 'With handwriting
we come closer to the intimacy of the
author,' Jouvent explains. . . . 'Each
person's hand is different: the gesture
is charged with emotion, lending it a
special charm'" (Chemin 2014).

coffee before students arrive, during a prep, or on the weekends. Some teachers prefer to have shorter sessions (five to ten minutes) daily, while others make time in longer stretches such as having a common meeting time in the company of colleagues.

BRAND YOUR BAD HANDWRITING

It would be wonderful if all the charts in the world could look like handwriting font exemplars, but no . . . our kids have us, not professional calligraphers, as teachers. Embrace your faulty scrawl and allow your class some time to learn how to read it. They will. We all have had a professor or parent whose handwriting we couldn't read at first but over time became clearer. In some ways, that moment when kids exclaim, "That's Mr. Jackson's handwriting!" actually forms a feeling of closeness, even a bond, that perfect handwriting cannot create. While of course we must strive to make our handwriting legible, we can also embrace its imperfections.

PHONE A FRIEND

It is no shame to consider outsourcing the work if no one can read your handwriting. One teacher we know asked his students to make the tools for him. In turn, he created an opportunity for them to access the work first and for the tools to truly be more student centered. Another teacher asked his wife to make his charts for him. (We can only assume that he did many chores for her during the week in repayment!) There is no shame in asking for help, as kids deserve to have the tools they need regardless of penmanship.

How (and Why) to Draw Effective Icons

The Nike swoosh . . . the rewind button . . . the red circle with a red slash through it. Small symbols convey big meaning. Using symbols or icons boosts the effectiveness of teaching tools because big ideas can be referenced in a small amount of space. Instead of a student needing to stop and read the phrase "consider the character's inner thinking," he instead can just glance up and see a thought bubble, an iconic representation of "thinking." Icons help cover a lot of ground quickly and are a natural way to communicate meaning and understand information. As Marjorie Martinelli and Kristine Mraz highlight in *Smarter Charts K–2*, "[kids] have been raised in a world filled with icons and images"

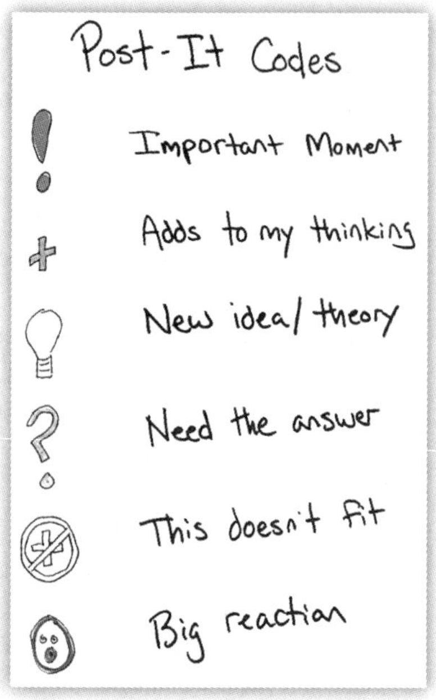

Figure 6–8 This shows some commonly used chart visuals. Check out Martinelli and Mraz's *Smarter Charts K–2* for quick lessons on drawing commonly used icons.

Figure 6-9 This symbolic word wall shows how pairing words or concepts with familiar visual icons creates associations for learning, building bridges from known to unknown information.

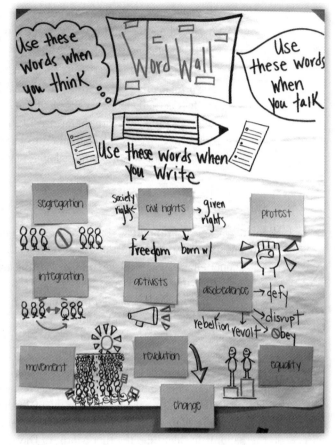

(2012). The quickest way to assess students' understanding, they argue, is to create an icon that represents some work and study how students take on that work with automaticity. Figure 6–8 shows a chart of commonly used icons (adapted from a similar list from Martinelli & Mraz 2012) to help students annotate quickly as they read.

Another way to use icons is harnessing their associative power. Not only can icons represent work, but they can create learning associations across a tool. For instance, when building students' vocabulary, pairing new words with familiar icons can help students learn the words by building associations between familiar knowledge and unknown terrain, as shown in Figure 6–9.

If you do not feel confident in your drawing skills, this can feel like tricky terrain. You might be imagining perfectly sketched eyes and ears for "look" and "listen," or bubble letter signs featured in a graphic novel. Instead, drawing helpful, clear icons can be as simple as drawing a question mark or a thought bubble. It's important that you don't feel alienated from this work simply because you lack a cartoonist's hand. Try these tips to create icons for your teaching tools:

- ☼ **Keep it simple.** Sometimes an exclamation point will do. Or a thought bubble. An icon is just a symbol, so make sure you focus on the symbols you already know how to create. When beginning this work, don't stray too far from what you can draw.

- ☼ **Use premade icons.** If you want to include icons that you know you can't draw yourself (or if, when you do include icons, your students ask why the elephant is eating that man and you reply, "That's an eye"), find someone who can make a few icons for you, or search clip art. Tape them to a sheet of paper, scan the sheet into a computer, and then print them on business labels for use on your teaching tools. This way you can have icons ready to go without stressing about the misinterpretation of your art.

☼ **Embrace your inner Picasso.** Hey, if Pablo can say that's a guitar, you can tell your kids that this is how you draw a stop sign. Martinelli and Mraz remind us, "It is actually more accessible if the end result resembles something your children could re-create themselves" (2012). The important thing about icons is that they are an agreed upon representation. If you and your class can agree that a squiggle means "Add dialogue to your writing," then that's what it means!

In Closing

In our Pinterest-saturated world, there is often an intense pressure to be able to craft like a ninja Martha Stewart. Education is not immune from this mindset. A quick online search for "anchor charts" will send you into an exciting and overwhelming sea of picture-perfect examples. These beautiful images might leave you feeling inspired and excited to make your own. But if you are like so many of us who are visually or artistically flawed, the barrage of perfect images can be quite daunting. To quote Marilyn Monroe, "I don't mind making jokes, but I don't want took like one." It's natural to want our teaching tools to look okay, and making visually appealing teaching tools is within reach for everyone. Use the tips in this chapter to help tap into your inner designer and artist. But in the end, it is far, far more important that teaching tools be helpful to kids, not attractive. When kids are involved in creating the tools, even in small ways, you'll cultivate a spirit of ownership and creativity that you just can't buy. As you dive in and begin creating tools, remember the handmade valentine, the first Mother's Day card made in art class, the birthday card your nephew made. What's most important is that teaching tools are creations with your students, flaws and all.

Afterword

We began this book with a story about a broken taillight and a truck full of. tools The tools allowed us to use Maggie's stepfather's knowledge of all things car related; they empowered us to do that which we could not do on our own. Sure, we saved some money in the process, but fixing the taillight did more than keep cash in our pockets. Walking away from the experience, we felt powerful, capable, and confident. There was one more thing that we had learned to do on our own in this world, one less thing we were dependent on others for. It felt good.

Our confidence was not born from the tools themselves; rather, it came from how Rich used them to teach us. He could have pointed to the tools in the truck and given us some simple directions, and perhaps we could have worked it out. Eventually, we would have figured out which tools worked for what, experimenting until we finally replaced the taillight (most likely along with many curse words, bruised thumbs, and broken parts along the way). But that's not what Rich did. Instead, he demonstrated how to use the ratchet to undo the bolts, how to jiggle the light fixture just so, so that it would come off without breaking the plastic tabs holding it in place. And then, most importantly, he replaced it all so we could do it ourselves. Because of his teaching, the way he showed us *how* to use the tools that could help us, our learning experience was fast and fulfilling and fun.

It's not just the content of a tool that transforms—here's a type of wrench or here's a micro-progression. Tools on their own are little more than ink and paper, wood and iron. The power of a tool depends on how it is used. Any tool can be used to help kids feel more empowered and confident, or more dependent and confused. We hope for the former. We hope that in this book we have helped you imagine the ways that teaching tools can help make your teaching feel more effective and efficient for you and your kids. We hope your teaching tools and the way you use them can feel like Rich and the taillight more often than not.

The tools we make and the way we use them communicate messages to our students. We like to think of them as personalized notes to students that say, "I see you, and I see your next steps as a reader, a writer, a thinker, a learner." Just as Rich imparts a bit of his wisdom by loaning a tool, we have opportunities to give our students gifts of our knowledge through the handwritten message a tool holds, like the theme Brandi Brown made in San Ramon, California, during her first year of teaching. Out of all the premade charts she could have bought at the teachers' store or all the behavioral or procedure charts she could have made detailing rules and routines, she instead opted to make and post the chart seen here, front and center in her classroom.

Brandi Brown's Chart

This was the message she wanted to share with her first class of middle schoolers—one of love, trust, and belief. Brandi reminds us that this can be an anthem that our tools sing out to students as they walk through our classroom doors. We can place things in front of students to lift them up and help them believe they can extend their reach, all the way to their dreams.

Appendix

Our Favorite Professional Texts Used When Finding and Writing Strategies for Teaching Tools

Here is a collection of our favorite professional texts—our sidekicks—that we use when finding and writing strategies for teaching tools.

General Reading Strategies

The Art of Slow Reading: Six Time-Honored Practices for Engagement
by Thomas Newkirk. 2012. Portsmouth, NH: Heinemann.

Falling in Love with Close Reading: Lessons for Analyzing Texts—and Life
by Christopher Lehman and Kate Roberts. 2014. Portsmouth, NH: Heinemann.

I Read It, but I Don't Get It: Comprehension Strategies for Adolescent Readers
by Cris Tovani. 2000. Portland, ME: Stenhouse Publishers.

The Reading Strategies Book: Your Everything Guide to Developing Skilled Readers
by Jennifer Serravallo. 2015. Portsmouth, NH: Heinemann.

Revisit, Reflect, Retell: Time-Tested Strategies for Teaching Reading Comprehension
by Linda Hoyt. 2009. Portsmouth, NH: Heinemann.

Strategies That Work: Teaching Comprehension to Enhance Understanding
by Stephanie Harvey and Anne Goudvis. 2000. York, ME: Stenhouse Publishers.

Teaching Reading in Middle School
by Laura Robb. 2000. New York: Scholastic Professional Books.

Units of Study for Teaching Reading: A Workshop Curriculum, Grades K–5
by Lucy Calkins et al. 2015. Portsmouth, NH: Heinemann.

Nonfiction Reading Strategies

Energize Research Reading and Writing: Fresh Strategies to Spark Interest, Develop Independence, and Meet Key Common Core Standards, Grades 4–8
by Christopher Lehman. 2012. Portsmouth, NH: Heinemann.

Making Sense of History: Using High-Quality Literature and Hands-On Experiences to Build Content Knowledge
by Myra Zarnowski. 2006. New York: Scholastic.

Nonfiction Matters: Reading, Writing, and Research in Grades 3–8
by Stephanie Harvey. 1998. York, ME: Stenhouse Publishers.

Reading Nonfiction: Notice and Note Stances, Signposts, and Strategies
by Kylene G. Beers and Robert E. Probst. 2015. Portsmouth, NH: Heinemann.

Subjects Matter: Every Teacher's Guide to Content-Area Reading
by Harvey Daniels and Steven Zemelman. 2014. Portsmouth, NH: Heinemann.

Teaching Reading in Social Studies, Science, and Math
by Laura Robb. 2003. New York: Scholastic Professional Books.

Texts and Lessons for Content-Area Reading
by Harvey Daniels and Nancy Steineke. 2011. Portsmouth, NH: Heinemann.

Interpretation and Analysis of Texts

Mosaic of Thought: The Power of Comprehension Strategy Instruction
by Ellin Oliver Keene and Susan Zimmermann. 2007. Portsmouth, NH: Heinemann.

Shades of Meaning: Comprehension and Interpretation in Middle School
by Donna Santman. 2005. Portsmouth, NH: Heinemann.

Teaching Interpretation: Using Text-based Evidence to Construct Meaning
by Sonja Cherry-Paul and Dana Johansen. 2014. Portsmouth, NH: Heinemann.

What Readers Really Do: Teaching Moves and Language to Match Process to Instruction
by Dorothy Barnhouse and Vicki Vinton. 2012. Portsmouth, NH: Heinemann.

What's the Big Idea? Question-Driven Units to Motivate Reading, Writing, and Thinking
by Jim Burke. 2010. Portsmouth, NH: Heinemann.

Emergent or Struggling Readers

The Fluent Reader: Oral and Silent Reading Strategies for Building Fluency, Word Recognition and Comprehension
by Timothy V. Rasinski. 2010. New York: Scholastic.

What Really Matters in Fluency: Research-Based Practices Across the Curriculum
by Richard L. Allington. 2009. Boston: Allyn and Bacon/Pearson.

What Research Has to Say about Reading Instruction
by Alan E. Farstrup and S. Jay Samuels. 2002. Newark, DE: International Reading Association.

When Kids Can't Read: What Teachers Can Do
by Kylene Beers. 2003. Portsmouth, NH: Heinemann.

Building a Reading Life

Book Love: Developing Depth, Stamina, and Passion in Adolescent Readers
by Penny Kittle. 2013. Portsmouth, NH: Heinemann.

The Book Whisperer: Awakening the Inner Reader in Every Child
by Donalyn Miller. 2009. San Francisco: Jossey-Bass.

Readicide: How Schools Are Killing Reading and What You Can Do About It
by Kelly Gallagher and Richard L. Allington. 2009. Portland, ME: Stenhouse Publishers.

Reading in the Wild: The Book Whisperer's Keys to Cultivating Lifelong Reading Habits
by Donalyn Miller and Susan Kelley. 2013. San Francisco: Jossey-Bass.

Writing About Reading

The Literary Essay: Analyzing Craft and Theme
by Kate Roberts and Katy Wischow. 2014. Units of Study in Argument, Information, and Narrative Writing, Grade 8. Portsmouth, NH: Heinemann.

Literary Essays: From Character to Compare/Contrast
by Lucy Calkins, Alexandra Marron, Kathleen Tolan, and Kate Roberts. 2014. Units of Study in Argument, Information, and Narrative Writing, Grade 6. Portsmouth, NH: Heinemann.

Notebook Connections: Strategies for the Reader's Notebook
by Aimee E. Buckner. 2009. Portland, ME: Stenhouse Publishers.

Talk to Literary Essays, Grades 3–8
by Janet Angelillo. 2003. Portsmouth, NH: Heinemann.

Writing About Reading: From Reader's Notebooks to Companion Books
by Lucy Calkins and Audra Kirshbaum Robb. 2014. Units of Study in Argument, Information, and Narrative Writing, Grade 7. Portsmouth, NH: Heinemann.

General Writing Strategies

The Art of Teaching Writing
by Lucy Calkins. 1986. Portsmouth, NH: Heinemann.

Assessing Writers
by Carl Anderson. 2005. Portsmouth, NH: Heinemann.

How's It Going? A Practical Guide to Conferring with Student Writers
by Carl Anderson. 2000. Portsmouth, NH: Heinemann.

Lessons That Change Writers
by Nancie Atwell. 2002. Portsmouth, NH: Heinemann.

On Writing Well: The Classic Guide to Writing Nonfiction
by William Zinsser. 2006. New York: HarperCollins.

The Resourceful Writing Teacher: A Handbook of Essential Skills and Strategies
by Jenny Mechem Bender. 2007. Portsmouth, NH: Heinemann.

The Revision Toolbox: Teaching Techniques That Work
by Georgia Heard. 2002. Portsmouth, NH: Heinemann.

The Unstoppable Writing Teacher: Real Strategies for the Real Classroom
by Colleen M. Cruz. 2015. Portsmouth, NH: Heinemann.

Writing Pathways: Performance Assessments and Learning Progressions, Grades K–8
by Lucy Calkins with Kelly Boland Hohne, Audra Kirshbaum Robb, and colleagues from
the Teachers College Reading and Writing Project. 2015. Portsmouth, NH: Heinemann.

Writing Tools: 50 Essential Strategies for Every Writer
by Roy Peter Clark. 2006. New York: Little, Brown and Company.

Writing with Mentors: How to Reach Every Writer in the Room Using Current, Engaging Mentor Texts
by Allison Marchetti and Rebekah O'Dell. 2015. Portsmouth, NH: Heinemann.

Units of Study in Opinion, Information, and Narrative Writing
by Lucy Calkins et al. 2013. Portsmouth, NH: Heinemann.

Writer's Craft Strategies

After the End: Teaching and Learning Creative Revision
by Barry Lane. 1993. Portsmouth, NH: Heinemann.

Awakening the Heart: Exploring Poetry in Elementary and Middle School
by Georgia Heard. 1999. Portsmouth, NH: Heinemann.

Craft Lessons: Teaching Writing K–8
by Ralph J. Fletcher and JoAnn Portalupi. 1998. York, ME: Stenhouse Publishers.

Dialogue: Techniques and Exercises for Crafting Effective Dialogue
by Gloria Kempton. 2004. Cincinnati, OH: Writer's Digest Books.

The Elements of Story: Field Notes on Nonfiction Writing
by Francis Flaherty. 2010. New York: Harper.

Finding the Heart of Nonfiction: Teaching 7 Essential Craft Tools with Mentor Texts
by Georgia Heard. 2013. Portsmouth, NH: Heinemann.

Now Write! Screenwriting: Exercises by Today's Best Writers and Teachers
by Sherry Ellis and Laurie Lamson. 2010. New York: Jeremy P. Tarcher/Penguin.

Plot and Structure: Techniques and Exercises for Crafting a Plot That Grips Readers from Start to Finish
by James Scott Bell. 2004. Cincinnati, OH: Writer's Digest Books.

What a Writer Needs
by Ralph J. Fletcher. 1993. Portsmouth, NH: Heinemann.

Wondrous Words: Writers and Writing in the Elementary Classroom
by Katie Wood Ray. 1999. Urbana, IL: National Council of Teachers of English.

Writers Are Readers: Flipping Reading Instruction into Writing Opportunities
by Lester L. Laminack and Reba M. Wadsworth. 2015. Portsmouth, NH: Heinemann.

Writing a Life: Teaching Memoir to Sharpen Insight, Shape Meaning— and Triumph over Tests
by Katherine Bomer. 2005. Portsmouth, NH: Heinemann.

Writing Fiction: A Guide to Narrative Craft
by Janet Burroway, Elizabeth Stuckey-French, and Ned Stuckey-French. 2011. Boston: Longman.

Conventions Usage

Catching Up on Conventions: Grammar Lessons for Middle School Writers
by Chantal Francois and Elisa Zonana. 2009. Portsmouth, NH: Heinemann.

The Elements of Style, 4th Edition
by William Strunk and E. B. White. 1999. London: Longman.

A Fresh Approach to Teaching Punctuation: Helping Young Writers Use Conventions with Precision and Purpose
by Janet Angelillo and Lucy Calkins. 2002. New York: Scholastic Professional Books.

The Glamour of Grammar: A Guide to the Magic and Mystery of Practical English
by Roy Peter Clark. 2010. New York: Little, Brown and Company.

Grammar Girl's Quick and Dirty Tips for Better Writing
by Mignon Fogarty. 2008. New York: Henry Holt.

The Power of Grammar: Unconventional Approaches to the Conventions of Language
by Mary Ehrenworth and Vicki Vinton. 2005. Portsmouth, NH: Heinemann.

Practical Punctuation: Lessons on Rule Making and Rule Breaking in Elementary Writing
by Daniel H. Feigelson. 2008. Portsmouth, NH: Heinemann.

A Vision and Inspiration for Charts: Content, Style, and Form

Chart Sense: Common Sense Charts to Teach 3–8 Informational Text and Literature
by Rozlyn Linder. 2014. Riverside, CA: The Literacy Initiative.

Chart Sense for Writing: Over 70 Common Sense Charts with Tips and Strategies to Teach 3–8 Writing
by Rozlyn Linder. 2015. Riverside, CA: The Literacy Initiative.

Smarter Charts for Math, Science and Social Studies: Making Learning Visible in the Content Areas
by Kristine Mraz and Majorie Martinelli. 2014. Portsmouth, NH: Heinemann.

Smarter Charts K–2: Optimizing an Instructional Staple to Create Independent Readers and Writers
by Marjorie Martinelli and Kristine Mraz. 2012. Portsmouth, NH: Heinemann.

References

Allen, David. 2001. *Getting Things Done: The Art of Stress-Free Productivity*. New York: Viking.

Applegate, Katherine. 2012. *The One and Only Ivan*. New York: Harper.

Beers, Kylene. 2003. *When Kids Can't Read: What Teachers Can Do*. Portsmouth, NH: Heinemann.

Beers, Kylene, and Robert E. Probst. 2015. *Reading Nonfiction: Notice and Note Stances, Signposts, and Strategies*. Portsmouth, NH: Heinemann.

———. 2014 "Rigor Without Relevance Is Simply Hard." *Twitter* (blog), November 6. https://twitter.com/kylenebeers/status/530456254461001728. Accessed September 3, 2015.

Bomer, Katherine. 2010. *Hidden Gems: Naming and Teaching from the Brilliance in Every Student's Writing*. Portsmouth, NH: Heinemann.

Bomer, Randy. 1995. *Time for Meaning: Crafting Literate Lives in Middle and High School*. Portsmouth, NH: Heinemann.

Calkins, Lucy. 1986. *The Art of Teaching Writing*. Portsmouth, NH: Heinemann.

———. 2001. *The Art of Teaching Reading*. New York: Longman.

Calkins, Lucy, et al. 2013. Units of Study in Opinion, Narrative, and Information Writing. Portsmouth, NH: Heinemann.

———. 2015. Units of Study for Teaching Reading: A Workshop Curriculum, Grades K–5. Portsmouth, NH: Heinemann.

Calkins, Lucy, with Kelly Boland Hohne, and Audra Kirshbaum Robb. 2015. *Writing Pathways: Performance Assessments and Learning Progressions, Grades K–8*. Portsmouth, NH: Heinemann.

Calkins, Lucy, Kelly Boland Hohne, and Cory Gillette. 2013. *Boxes and Bullets: Personal and Persuasive Essays*. Units of Study in Opinion, Information, and Narrative Writing, Grade 4. Portsmouth, NH: Heinemann.

Carey, Benedict. 2015. *How We Learn: Throw Out the Rule Book and Unlock Your Brain's Potential*. London: Pan Books.

Chemin, Anne. 2014. "Handwriting vs Typing: Is the Pen Still Mightier than the Keyboard?" *The Guardian* (London), December 16.

Council of Chief State School Officers, and National Governors Association. n.d. *Supplemental Information for Appendix A of the Common Core State Standards for English Language Arts and Literacy: New Research on Text Complexity*. https://d1jt5u2s0h3gkt.cloudfront.net/m/cms_page_media/135/E0813_Appendix_A_New_Research_on_Text_Complexity.pdf.

Cruz, M. Colleen. 2015. *The Unstoppable Writing Teacher: Real Strategies for the Real Classroom*. Portsmouth, NH: Heinemann.

Dean, Jeremy. 2013. *Making Habits, Breaking Habits: Why We Do Things, Why We Don't, and How to Make Any Change Stick*. Richmond, VA: Oneworld.

DiCamillo, Kate. 2001. *The Tiger Rising*. Cambridge, MA: Candlewick Press.

Dweck, Carol S. 2006. *Mindset: The New Psychology of Success*. New York: Random House.

Ehrenworth, Mary, and Vicki Vinton. 2005. *The Power of Grammar: Unconventional Approaches to the Conventions of Language*. Portsmouth, NH: Heinemann.

Fletcher, Ralph J., and JoAnn Portalupi. 1998. *Craft Lessons: Teaching Writing K–8*. York, ME: Stenhouse Publishers.

Francois, Chantal, and Elisa Zonana. 2009. *Catching Up on Conventions: Grammar Lessons for Middle School Writers*. Portsmouth, NH: Heinemann.

Gazzaniga, Michael S. 2009. *The Cognitive Neurosciences*. 4th edition. Cambridge, MA: MIT Press.

Harvey, Stephanie, and Anne Goudvis. 2000. *Strategies That Work: Teaching Comprehension to Enhance Understanding*. York, ME: Stenhouse Publishers.

Hattie, John. 2009. *Visible Learning: A Synthesis of Over 800 Meta-analyses Relating to Achievement*. London: Routledge.

Heard, Georgia. 2002. *The Revision Toolbox: Teaching Techniques That Work*. Portsmouth, NH: Heinemann.

Hicks, Troy. 2009. *The Digital Writing Workshop*. Portsmouth, NH: Heinemann.

Keene, Ellin Oliver, and Susan Zimmermann. 1997. *Mosaic of Thought: Teaching Comprehension in a Reader's Workshop*. Portsmouth, NH: Heinemann.

Kittle, Penny. 2013. *Book Love: Developing Depth, Stamina, and Passion in Adolescent Readers*. Portsmouth, NH: Heinemann.

Klauser, Henriette Anne. 2001. *Write It Down, Make It Happen: Knowing What You Want—and Getting It!* New York: Scribner.

Lehman, Christopher. 2012. *Energize Research Reading and Writing: Fresh Strategies to Spark Interest, Develop Independence, and Meet Key Common Core Standards, Grades 4–8*. Portsmouth, NH: Heinemann.

Lin, D. Y. M. 2004. "Evaluating Older Adults' Retention in Hypertext Perusal: Impacts of Presentation Media as a Function of Text Topology." *Computers in Human Behavior*, 20.

Macon, James M., Diane Bewell, and MaryEllen Vogt. 1991. *Responses to Literature: Grades K–8*. Newark, DE: International Reading Association.

Martinelli, Marjorie, and Kristine Mraz. 2012. *Smarter Charts K–2: Optimizing an Instructional Staple to Create Independent Readers and Writers*. Portsmouth, NH: Heinemann.

Miller, Donalyn, and Susan Kelley. 2013. *Reading in the Wild: The Book Whisperer's Keys to Cultivating Lifelong Reading Habits*. San Francisco: Jossey-Bass.

Mraz, Kristine, and Majorie Martinelli. 2014. *Smarter Charts for Math, Science, and Social Studies: Making Learning Visible in the Content Areas*. Portsmouth, NH: Heinemann.

Ness, Patrick. 2008. *The Knife of Never Letting Go*. Cambridge, MA: Candlewick Press.

Palacio, R. J. 2012. *Wonder*. New York: Knopf Books for Young Readers.

Pearson, P. David, Laura R. Roehler, Janice A. Dole, and Gerald G. Duffy. 1992. "Developing Expertise in Reading Comprehension." In *What Research Has to Say About Reading Instruction*, edited by Alan E. Farstrup and S. Jay Samuels, 145–99. 2nd edition. Newark, DE: International Reading Association.

Pink, Daniel H. 2009. *Drive: The Surprising Truth About What Motivates Us*. New York: Riverhead Books.

Pransky, Ken. 2010. "The Multidimensional Vocabulary Crisis and Ways to Address It." http://www.readingandwritingproject.com/public/resources/workshop_materials/10-20-2010/pransky/vocab_notes.pdf. Accessed September 3, 2015.

Rami, Meenoo. 2014. *Thrive: 5 Ways to (Re)Invigorate Your Teaching*. Portsmouth, NH: Heinemann.

Ray, Katie Wood. 1999. *Wondrous Words: Writers and Writing in the Elementary Classroom*. Urbana, IL: National Council of Teachers of English.

Schwartz, Shanna. 2008. *A Quick Guide to Making Your Teaching Stick, K–5*. Portsmouth, NH: Heinemann.

Serravallo, Jennifer. 2015. *The Reading Strategies Book: Your Everything Guide to Developing Skilled Readers*. Portsmouth, NH: Heinemann.

Snow, Richard, and Marshall Farr. 1987. *Aptitude, Learning, and Instruction. Vol. 3, Conative and Affective Process Analyses*. Hillsdale, NJ: Lawrence Erlbaum Associates.

Tomlinson, Carol A. 1999. *The Differentiated Classroom: Responding to the Needs of All Learners*. Alexandria, VA: Association for Supervision and Curriculum Development.